BRIDGING MINDSET GAPS

Dr. Tom Hallquist

ISBN 978-1-64468-976-9 (Paperback)
ISBN 978-1-64468-977-6 (Digital)

Publisher's Cataloging-In-Publication Data
(Prepared by The Donohue Group, Inc.)

Names: Hallquist, Tom, Dr., author.
Title: Bridging mindset gaps: perceptions of education and the influence on criminal activity /
Dr. Tom Hallquist.
Description: First edition. | Murrells Inlet, SC: Covenant Books, Inc., [2020] | A revision
of the author's dissertation (doctoral)—Middle Tennessee State University, 2019. | Includes
bibliographical references and index.
Identifiers: ISBN 9781644689769 (paperback) | ISBN 9781644689776 (digital)
Subjects: LCSH: Education and crime. | Prisoners—Attitudes. | Recidivism—Prevention. |
Organizational change. | Coevolution—Social aspects.
Classification: LCC HV6166 .H35 2020 (print) | LCC HV6166 (ebook) | DDC 364.25—dc23

Covenant Books, Inc.
11661 Hwy 707
Murrells Inlet, SC 29576
www.covenantbooks.com

ACKNOWLEDGMENTS

I am indebted to the women and men who are and have been incarcerated and have willingly participated in this research to allow me to share their experiences in order to make a difference in the lives of others. I am extremely grateful to the faculty and staff of Middle Tennessee State University, especially Dr. Rick Vanosdall, for the guidance and support in this journey. I appreciate my committee Dr. Kevin Krahenbuhl, Dr. Gary Kiltz, and Dr. Lando Carter for their patience and advice by demanding more than what is expected. I also want to thank Julie Haun-Frank for her support and guidance. Cohort 3 of the ALSI doctoral program has been a tremendous benefit by supplying support and encouragement. I also want to thank the Davidson County Sheriff's Office, especially Paul Mulloy and Tiffany Manning, for their encouragement and assistance. I personally want to thank Dr. Lacey Benns, Dr. Tom Flagel, and Dr. Candace Warner from Columbia State Community College and Dr. Mary Vaughn and Dr. Nathan Webb from Belmont University for their encouragement in this endeavor. I want to also thank Dr. Leta Frazier and Phil Frazier from Bethel University for believing in me and encouraging me to pursue a career in education and introducing me to the importance of an "I–Thou" experience. With deep appreciation and want to thank Dr. John P. Kotter, Professor Emeritus, Harvard School of Business and Dr. Douglas Reeves, founder of the Center for Successful Leadership for the guidance and support in this endeavor. Finally, I want to thank my relatives and friends, especially my wife, Wesley Ann, and my daughters, Katie and Annie, for their understanding and patience throughout this incredible ordeal.

ABSTRACT

The purpose of this narrative research is to develop an understanding of the mindset of the incarcerated individual towards education and if the experience had an impact on criminal activity. By understanding the mindset, research questions and solutions can be developed that will have the greatest impact on a course of action in deterring criminal behavior. If one can determine the main problems and narrow the list to the ones that could potentially be solved, then one can develop meaningful questions and establish a clear and concise purpose for the framework of prevention. In discussing the problems within the educational system, one must consider the possible nature of the initial problems and the effects they have on those prone to incarceration. The focus of this study was to develop a foundation for further research in educational experiences of inmates and to develop an awareness of the impact teachers and administrators have on students and potentially create the importance of positive interactions on influencing future behavior and actions. In addition, this research project may change the mindset of inmates so they can be released back into society and have a positive impact on the community. The implementation of the principles in this research can also be applied to public and private schools, community development projects, organization leadership in business, the family structure, and the self-centered individual.

CONTENTS

LIST OF TABLES

LIST OF FIGURES

CHAPTER 1

Introduction to Research

The purpose of this narrative research is to develop an understanding of the mindset of the incarcerated individual toward education and if the experience had an impact on criminal activity. By understanding the mindset, research questions and solutions can be developed that will have the greatest impact on a course of action in deterring criminal behavior. The focus of the research questions was on meaning, influence, and the process as described in Joseph Maxwell's book *Qualitative Research Design: An Interpretative Approach*, 2nd Edition (Maxwell, 75). If one can determine the main problems and narrow the list to the ones that could potentially be solved, then one can develop meaningful questions and establish a clear and concise purpose for the framework of prevention. In discussing the problems within the educational system, one must consider the possible nature of the initial problems and the effects they have on those prone to incarceration. The focus of this study was to develop a foundation for further research in educational experiences of inmates and to develop an awareness of the impact teachers and administrators have on students and potentially create the importance of positive interactions on influencing future behavior and actions. In addition, this research project may change the mindset of inmates so they can be released back into society and have a positive impact on the community. The concern for the Department of Corrections and society is not just the level of education of the incarcerated individual but also the recidivism rate for inmates who have been released back into society. Recidivism is defined as an individual who is arrested for committing a crime after initially being released from jail or prison. The data collected is further explained.

Context

This study examines the perceptions of inmates of their public education experiences and the possible influence these perceptions had on their criminal activities that lead to incarceration. As reported by the DCSO, 76 percent of the inmates have not received a high school diploma. The values of this study was to establish if there was a relationship between education and criminal behavior that led to incarceration. The study will be conducted at a large midsouth state's County Sheriff's Department jail facility and a maximum-security state prison. The county jail has a capacity of 2,400 inmates with up to 35,000 bookings per year. The stay in the facility ranges from one day to two years. The educational courses available include the High School Equivalency Test (HiSET) process where an individual can earn a high school equivalency credential diploma. The Comprehensive Adult Student Assessment System (CASAS) is used to assess adult basic needs in reading, math, and language arts abilities. Other programs range from anger management to life skills and drug counseling to religious studies. The state has a population of just over 6.7 million inhabitants with a state prison system that houses over 22,000 inmates in eleven facilities and supervises over 76,000 parolees back into the community.

The DOC prison system offers educational programs in HiSET and offers courses in vocational training, such as construction, engine repair, and culinary arts. The National Center for Construction Education and Research (NCCER) offers a standardized curriculum complete with reentry and journey-level written assessments as part of the National Craft Assessment and Certification Program (NCACP). The study was conducted at the county Sheriff's Department jail facility and parolees from the state prison facilities during a three-month period in the summer and early fall of 2018. There were fifteen to twenty women participants in the HiSET diploma program and the curriculum established a sense of purpose not only for the study but also for the students. The men who participated were recently paroled from the Department of Corrections and had been involved in previous Parenting from Prison classes that were conducted by this researcher. The importance of this course of action was that it established a rapport of trust between the researcher and the students.

A pilot study was initiated to determine the feasibility of the research question and establish guidelines for further research. The study was beneficial in that it provided insight to the thought processes of inmates and gave an opportunity to revise the questions and procedures for the main research question. Focus groups sessions were held on February 20 and 27, 2017, to determine the relationship between the school experience and criminal activity. The pilot study results indicated that there was a relationship between school educational experiences and criminal activity. The study results are included in chapter 3 of this dissertation.

Statement of the Problem

Christian Henrichson and Ruth Delaney wrote in a report to the Vera Institute of Justice, "The Price of Prisons: What Incarceration Costs Taxpayers" (2013):

> A growing body of research suggests—and government officials acknowledge—that beyond a certain point, further increases in incarceration have significantly diminishing returns as a means of making communities safer. This means that for many systems, putting lower-risk offenders in prison is yielding increasingly smaller improvements in public safety and may cost more to taxpayers than the value of the crime it prevents. As states look to strike a balance that results in better outcomes, it is essential to assess the benefits and costs of incarceration. (p.12)

While there has been much written about the cost factors and inmate attitudes toward educational programming while being incarcerated, there has been few to no studies exploring the incarcerated inmate perception of their school educational experience to their criminal behavior that led to incarceration within the County Sheriff's Office. This research focused on the problems that (1) traditional education does not work for everyone, (2) patterns of inequity in demographics and academic achievement, and (3) the impact of perceptions that lead to increased proclivity to engage in criminal behavior, and (4) societal influence from family, community, peers, and self. Richard S. Baskas, a specialist for the Department of Justice, wrote an article "Inmates' Attitudes toward Pre-Release Educational and Vocational Programs" for the department, which states that there is a mixed attitude among inmates about the effectiveness of the programs:

Inmates share both positive and negative attitudes with regards to pre-release educational and vocational programs in federal and state prison institutions. To a degree prison staff can provide more opportunities to improve inmates' attitudes towards pre-release educational and vocational programs within the combines of the prison environment. (pp. 2–7)

The importance of this study is that it examines the failure of society to fully comprehend the importance of education and the effect is has on criminal behavior. The problem could be the attitude toward rehabilitation and penance in correctional facilities. Muriel Schmid explains in her book *The Eye of God* that the religious beliefs of the Pennsylvania Quakers in the sixteenth century helped developed prison reform policies and the architectural design of the prisons. The first US penitentiary was built in Pennsylvania in 1796 with the philosophy that solitary confinement would best accomplish the reforms of the criminal mindset through reflection and spiritual meditation. The penitentiary was designed like a European monastery with small cells with a window or sky-light that was to remind the inmate that God was watching. The belief was that criminals would be reformed by being incarcerated in a massive overbearing prison structure with small cells and a spiritual transformation "leading them from law to grace, from sin to forgiveness, and finally from death to life" (pp. 553–554). This penance mindset still prevails today, not only by the Department of Corrections but by society demanding penance. Does the system work? should be the question. Per the US Bureau of Justice Statistics,

> 2,239,800 adults were incarcerated in U.S. federal, state prisons, and county jails by the beginning 2013. Additionally, approximately 4,814,200 adults at the beginning of 2013 were on probation or parole. In total, 6.98 million adults were under correctional supervision either by probation, parole, jail, or in prison or about 2.9% of adults in the U.S. resident population.

In addition, there were over 70,000 juveniles in juvenile detention centers. An article, "Recidivism of Prisoners Released in 30 States in 2005: Patterns from 2005 to 2010," by Cooper, Durose, and Snyder reports that

> within three years of release, 67.8% of former prisoners are rearrested and within 5 years of release, 84.1% of inmates who were age 24 or younger at release were arrested, compared to 78.6% of inmates ages 25 to 39 and 69.2% of those inmates age 40 or older. (Cooper 2014, 1–31)

The statistical data are disturbing and further reenforces that societal issues of demographics, privilege, economics and that penance does not work. But what can be done? Has public education failed a large segment of society? According to Libby Nelson and Dara Lind in their article "The School to Prison Pipeline, Explained," students who are suspended are more likely to repeat a grade or drop out of school. Per US Census data in 2011, there were 776,952 high school dropouts aged twenty-five or older living in the state. "This group represents most residents who are either unemployed, in need of Medicaid assistance, or incarcerated. The data show that as the general level of education increases (from associate degree to bachelor's degree and so forth), the use of public assistance programs declines," reports the author Christian D'Andrea in an article for the

Foundation for Educational Choice, entitled "Tennessee's High School Dropouts: Examining the Fiscal Consequences" (2010, 5–15).

The authors of "An Examination of the Basic Reading Skills of Incarcerated Males" stipulate that male prisoners in the United States have a fifth-grade equivalency for reading. Margret Shippers, the primary author, states that providing evidence-based literacy training must be a national priority (pp. 4–12). As disturbing as these statistics are, what is often ignored by the criminal justice system in the United States is the relationship between inmates, their families, and the role education. Many women and men in prison are parents of children under the age of eighteen. There are many issues that arise when a parent is incarcerated, situations ranging from financial, legal, and emotional. What is often overlooked is how children are impacted. It is often stated that when a parent is incarcerated, the children also "do the time," implies L. Glaze, and L. Maruschak in their article "Parents in Prison and Their Minor Children" (2008). Although many children who have a parent in prison adjust and go on to live very successful lives, it must be noted that children who have parents in prison are more likely to have difficulty in school, both academically and socially, reported Creaslie Hairston in an article "Focus on Children with Incarcerated Parents" (2007, 20).

Children who have a parent in prison are more likely to engage in substance abuse, delinquency, and gang-related activities. Sixty-three percent of youth suicides are from fatherless homes or five times the national average, per the US Department of Health/Census. The Center for Disease Control reports that 85 percent of children from fatherless homes have behavior disorders. The National Principles Association states that 71 percent of high school dropouts come from fatherless homes. Ninety percent of homeless and runaway children and 71 percent of teenage pregnancy are from fatherless homes. Seventy-five percent of adolescent patients in chemical abuse centers come from fatherless homes. With a father incarcerated, the child doubles the risk of physical, emotional, or educational neglect.

Daughters with an incarcerated father are 53 percent more likely to marry as teenagers, 71 percent more likely to have children as teenagers, and 92 percent more likely to get divorced (p. 1). Children of incarcerated parents are 71 percent more likely to be incarcerated themselves than children from a family-based support culture. These statistics are from the US Department of Health and Human Services Census Report (p.1). Nancy La Vigne, Elizabeth, Davis, and Diana Brazzell offer further insights to the problems facing children of incarcerated parents in an article written for the Urban Justice Policy Center, "Broken Bonds: Understanding and Addressing the Needs of Children with Incarcerated Parents." The authors state that over 1.5 million children have incarcerated parents (2008, 1–14).

> In interviews with 58 incarcerated mothers, school performance problems, including poor grades, truancy, suspensions and poor behavior at school and at home, were identified as the major problems their children were experiencing. (Hairston 2007, 20)

Another major problem that is not aligned with this study that must be addressed is economics or the cost of incarceration which poses a burden on taxpayers. An article in the *Federal Register*, a daily journal of the US, stipulates that the "average cost of incarceration for Federal inmates in Fiscal Year 2011 was $28,893.40. The average annual cost to confine an inmate in a Community Corrections Center for Fiscal Year 2011 was $26,163," per the director of the Bureau of Prisons, Charles E. Samuels. In comparison to public education expenditures, the average cost per student for elementary education in the year 2013 was $10,702. In this state, the expenditure for public education is $8,208 per student. The data regarding educational expenditures came from the US Census Bureau Public Education Finances Report, 2013.

The data ranging from the present recidivism rate to the effect on the children of the incarcerated and the cost of the cost of incarceration versus education shows a possible discrepancy in the thought process toward the importance of education and the possible reduction of the recidivism rate for ex-offenders. This study considered the following research questions:

1) The primary research question was to determine if the public school education system had and influenced incarcerated individuals criminal activities?
2) If there was an influence, then other research problems for this study was to determine if there are more efficient methods that could have been utilized by the school district to develop better educational opportunities for men and women?
3) What are the challenges facing not only the school district but also the students?
4) What role did one's educational experience have on criminal behavior?
5) What opportunities were there in school and for the inmates to better their educational experience?
6) What could have been done differently in school to impact your decision for criminal behavior to be incarcerated in the County Sheriff's Office jail facilities?
7) Was the learning process in school similar to the learning process of the incarcerated individual?
8) What were other influences besides education that led to criminal behavior?

Some of these questions are answered in the interview process, and others are designed for future research. The focus for this research is the influence of public education on criminal activity. This researcher felt it was imperative to also study the educational system in the prison system to establish a foundation of knowledge and understanding of the mindsets of the educational format and of the incarcerated individual. For the DOC and the county jail facilities, educational programs offer a High School Equivalency (HiSET) classes for court-ordered inmates who want to further their education. With the limited resources, the program is trying hard to offer excellent educational opportunities, and they are succeeding under the guidelines of the Sheriff's Department. But the problem is the statistical importance of reporting the data of High School Equivalency Diploma (HiSET) graduates as a benchmark that the educational programs are working and reducing the rate of recidivism. The statistical analysis should be dramatically improved. The present assessment utilized by the Sheriff's Office is designed to teach to the test by giving sample pre-HiSET informative tests to the students to learn the answers so they are familiar with the final state examination. The question is, what are they actually learning? They are learning the answers to a test, but not the significance of the subject.

The present pre-HiSET test is easy to administer by computer programs for self-study or by teachers lecturing about the subject matter, then discussing the questions by giving the student the correct answer. Hopefully, the student will memorize the answer to the question. There is little to no instruction as to the process of determining the correct answer. The purpose of the jail facility is to graduate as many students to show an indication of success for the program. But is presenting diplomas at the expense of a quality educational experience designed for success? In a policy information report, "Locked Up and Lock Out: An Educational Perspective on the US Prison Population," authors Richard Coley and Paul Burton stipulate that the rate of recidivism is reduced due to the length and integrity of educational programs (p. 22). There are philosophical differences; the sheriff's obligation is to graduate as many students in the shortest period, not really concerned with the quality of education.

One factor that enhances this philosophy is that inmates in the jail system can have a relatively short stay before being transferred to another prison facility or released on bail. This makes educational programing difficult to administer. An additional research question is the similarities between public school education and the format used by the prison system. One of the major problems facing in the Sheriff's Office and the Department of Corrections is funding for educational programs. According to the director of Programing for the Sheriff's Department, the money that is allocated for educational programs comes from grants and is relatively insufficient to administer a proper HiSET program. The instructors are poorly paid and, in some cases, do not have teacher certifications to teach. The utilization of volunteers, college interns, and professors have helped offset financial expenditures. This is a problem that must be addressed not only the legislature but by the general population to allocate more funding toward rehabilitation. The general population must be made aware of the present conditions of prison education and the potential for initiating a positive change in rehabilitative philosophies. John H. Esperian's article "The Effect of Prison Education Programs on Recidivism," in a report to the *Journal of Correctional Education* in December 2010, stated that cost to educate inmates offsets the cost of incarceration due to the lowering of the recidivism rate (p.333).

Purpose of the Study

The purpose of this study is to develop a foundation for further study to see if there is a relationship between school education experiences and criminal activity of the incarcerated individual. This study emphasized the inmate perception of their educational experience in the public school system and not based on education in general due to only one individual having attended a private school. That individual was arrested for drug crimes of usage. Ironically, she was an AP student in a private high school academy, and when tested for grade-level equivalency in math, she tested at a first-grade level. The premise is to see if there is a relationship between public school education experiences and criminal behavior. If there is a relationship, then alternative approaches may be developed to improve the situation, and new approaches may be incorporated into the educational system in both the public school system and in the educational programs in the jail and prison systems.

The findings of this research may be used to design a format to assist in changing the mindset of the individual and emphasize the importance of education to develop positive interactions and break the cycle of children following their parents to prison. Being incarcerated does not mean one must give up rights to be a role model or that the relationship with their children becomes less important. It allows one the opportunity to become a positive mentor and role model for their children and for society. The anticipated outcome is to establish accountability and credibility within the individual and include the family structure or even create a new family organizational format. By understanding the past and present conditions, one can begin to develop a strategy to initiate change and develop a new purpose for education besides getting a job.

Can a practical, purposeful, and value-orientated curriculum have a positive effect on the rate of recidivism and help change the system from penance to rehabilitation? Previously stated, money for educational programs comes from grants, volunteer organization, and not an expenditure from the state budget, per the director of Programing for the Sheriff's Office. The Sheriff's Office offers limited programs, but not in the traditional educational manner of the public school system. This offers a challenge different from conventional or traditional educational systems but also allows for the initiation of new programing that will enhance the skills of the individuals who are incarcerated.

Research Questions

What are the perceptions of inmates of educational experiences in the public school educational system, and what influence it had on their criminal activity? This is important to the actualization that public schools had an influence on criminal activity, but there are other factors gathered from this research that are related to the cause of criminal behavior. Factors such as family, community, peer pressure, and economics were also be the contributing agents that led to incarceration. The focus is the influence of public school education, but the narrative inquiry leads to further clarification for criminal behavior and offers solutions to correct the present situation, not only in education but other contributing influences. What are the attitudes toward the purpose of education for the students in the public school environment? If the educational influence is prevalent in public education, could this same attitude be prevalent in the correctional educational programs? Can motivational theories be introduced into the programs that will enhance the educational experience by making educators aware of the circumstances and to initiate change in the mindset of incarcerated individual and the teacher? By researching these basic questions of the inmate's reflection on education, the researcher was able to develop a course of action for further implementation of effective purpose-driven educational programs, as explained in chapter 5 of this research.

Overview of Present Conditions in Relation to the Research Question

The present educational conditions in relation to the research question were initiated by the use of an equity audit of the demographics of the community, as well as an academic achievement audit of the inner-city school system from where the majority of inmates attended school. The findings are reported in chapter 4 of this research. In summary of the academic audits, the findings indicated a large gap in comprehension, reading, and math and the grade level reported. The audit also indicates the segregation of the communities and the location of criminal behavior. The present conditions to the research question also include county jail educational programs. The mission statement for the County Sheriff's Office is, "As a law enforcement agency committed to public safety, we strive to be a leader in the field of corrections, service of civil process, and innovative community-based programs emphasizing Accountability, Diversity, Integrity, Professionalism."

Within the organizational structure of the Sheriff's Office, an educational section has been established to assist inmates receive a high school equivalency diploma while they are incarcerated and after they have been released from jail. As previously stated, the main difficulty is that there is little financial assistance from the county or state to develop an effective educational program. There is no major emphasis by society, governmental officials, or the Department of Corrections on the benefits of educational programs for the incarcerated. A secondary potential outcome of this study is to redefine the importance of education as a device to prevent incarceration and to deter the recidivism rate for individuals who have been incarcerated by the county. This would also include the potential to break the family cycle of criminal behavior and incarceration. Once inmates can motivate themselves to excel in education and prove their worth to society, then there would motivation by society to develop programs of rehabilitation. The starting place to initiate change is by understanding the mindset of the inmate.

Significance of the Study

This research study is to determine if there is an influence of public education on criminal activity of incarcerated individuals. If the findings indicate that public education influences criminal activity, then this concept calls for support from the community, government officials, Department of Corrections administrators, as well as students. This study could also result in other findings, such as lack of family involvement, peer pressure, cultural differences, and the self-actualization of purpose, or the feeling of hopefulness that are contributing causes of criminal activity. The mindset of penance over rehabilitation must be addressed, and the quality of our public educational system must be reviewed. The academic-achievement gap between inner city and affluent school systems must be addressed, if findings from this research indicate that education does have a direct role in criminal activities. There must be public forums discussing the problems and consequences and offering solutions.

Conceptual Framework

A *narrative inquiry* "seeks not just to understand, but also to build a substantive theory about the phenomenon of interest" (*Merriam* 2009, 23). The foundation for this study will be the utilization of the narrative inquiry with the rationale of not wanting to test the established theory of educational reform but to understand the *why* of how our educational programing is functioning as it is and to develop a new format of practical, purpose, and value-driven educational rehabilitation reform. The conceptual framework has many manifolds that could lead to the development of awareness for educational reform in public education, the prison, and jail systems. The first conceptual framework is to listen to the perceptions of the inmates to establish if there is a need for educational reform. Second is to develop a narrative to further explain the findings so societies can comprehend the need for rehabilitative reform by understanding the benefits of such reform. If the findings indicate a problem or condition exists in the educational system, then with society's knowledge and demand for reform, the legislative can be pressured to enact initiatives to create change. With the legislative support and backing, the Department of Corrections can develop meaningful and purpose-driven educational programs.

Definition of Terms and Abbreviations

AIMS. Advanced Instructional Management System.

AutoSkill. Component reading subskills program, which was reportedly designed to teach cognitive subskills of reading.

CASAS. Comprehensive Adult Student Assessment System. CASAS is a nonprofit organization that focuses on assessment and curriculum development of basic skills for youth and adults. CASAS programs are used by federal and state government agencies, business and industry, community colleges, education and training providers, correctional facilities (https://www.casas.org).

CASEL. The Collaborative for Academic, Social, and Emotional Learning.

DOC. Department of Corrections.

EOCA. Equity-Oriented Change Agent.

GED. General Educational Development. GED tests are a group of four-subject tests that, when passed, certify that the test taker has American or Canadian high school–level academic skills. The General Equivalency Diploma provides certification of high school academic standards (https://ged.com).

HiSET. The HiSET (High School Equivalency Test) is an assessment of skills and knowledge comparable to those of a high school graduate. The HiSET test is a series of five tests covering writing, science, math, literature and the arts, and social studies. These tests require the test taker to apply reading, math, language, and critical-thinking skills. Passing the HiSET test series allows student to earn their High School Equivalency Diploma (HSED) (https://www.dmacc.edu/hiset/Pages/welcome.aspx).

Incarcerated students. According to 34 CFR 600.2 [Title 34—Education; Subtitle B-Regulations of the Offices of the Department of Education; Chapter VI—Office of Postsecondary Education, Department of Education; Part 600—Institutional Eligibility under the Higher Education Act of 1965, as Amended; Subpart A—General], the term *incarcerated student* means "a student who is serving a criminal sentence in a Federal, State, or local penitentiary, prison, jail, reformatory, work farm, or other similar correctional institution. A student is not considered incarcerated if that student is in a half-way house or home detention or is sentenced to serve only weekends" (https://definitions.uslegal.com/i/incarcerated-student-education/).

NCACP. National Craft Assessment and Certification Program.

NCCER. National Center for Construction Education and Research.

PLATO. Programmed Logic for Automatic Teaching Operations. An instructional software package for mathematics, reading, and language.(http://faculty.coe.uh.edu/smcneil/cuin6373/idhistory/plato.html).

Recidivism. "A tendency to relapse into a previous condition or mode of behavior; *especially*: relapse into criminal behavior" (https://www.merriam-webster.com/dictionary/recidivism).

SEL. Social Emotional Learning (CASEL).

TABE9/10 D Survey. Use TABE to evaluate the reading, mathematics, and language skill levels of students or trainees. The results will help place each person in the appropriate instructional or training program and track progress toward success (http://tabetest.com/students-2/tabe-910/ D).

Limitations

The purpose of this narrative research is to determine if public education influenced criminal activity of incarcerated individuals. Most of the studies that were reviewed and focused on prison or jail educational programs and the positive effectiveness of the programs as perceived by the students and administrators. An extensive research of academic data bases, periodicals, dissertation abstracts, and online articles found little on the influence of public education and criminal activity. The lack of this research limits the direction of this study but allows for creativity and innovation. Limitations in this study refer to the physical and social environments of prison life, including different educational programs and the inability to gather data from different correctional databases.

The quantitative analysis data comes from several sources and the information is not compatible or cannot be interconnected with other databases. There is also a lack of interconnectivity of data between different educational programs ranging from the PLATO learning program, HiSET, GED, and CASAS training systems. Databases had to be developed to access information on the final grade attended, grade equivalency, and recidivism rate for inmates participating in the educational programs. These databases were initiated but cannot be validated due to the short period of time of activation. Validation will be developed by initially linking different databases to gather information and then incorporating one standard and source for future analysis. The validation of the information must be over a period that develops credibility and reliability of accuracy. The prison mindset of the individual must be considered in answering the research questions and be able to interpret the answers or motive for the answers.

This limitation is the prison environment, including prison personnel, administrators, and guards. The rules and regulations in prison are different than a research project in an atmosphere of normality outside of the prison walls and barbed-wire fences. Strict time allotment is enforced but could change due to lockdowns. Participants could be withdrawn from the study due to behavior issues, transferred to another facility, and pardoned or released from prison. Another limitation is the lack of interactions between researcher and the participants. There is no physical contact to be made between inmates and teachers, including handshakes or a pat on the back. The atmosphere within the prison system is that penance and rehabilitation are not considered the true function of the facility.

Another major limitation is the limited use of quantitative statistics. The quantitative statistics in this research is used to develop a foundation of understanding and appreciation for the qualitative study and the use of generalizability. According to Joseph Maxwell in his book *Qualitative Research Design*, "external generalizability refers to the ability to apply the findings from this study to other individuals and contexts" (Maxwell 2005, 115). Sharan Merriam in her book *Qualitative Research: A Guide to Design and Implementation* stipulates that "the statistical sense cannot occur in qualitative research" (Merriam 2009, 224). Merriam explained that qualitative researchers are concerned with "transferability or external validity" (p. 239). The intent is to limit the quantitative research and focus on the sufficient descriptive narrative data so that practitioners and researchers can make choices based on observation and develop a transformative curiosity to conduct further research. The quantitative data is used to develop a foundation of knowledge, understanding, and appreciation for all concerned.

Delimitations

Delimitations are variables that is purposefully left out or placed in the research. The first delimitation was the choice of the problem and limiting the scope to the research question. The environmental conditions of the prison and jail facilities have been purposely left out of this research project. The present mindset of the individual participants was considered, but not the focus of this research project, but could be included in the findings to offer a solution. The focus was on the perceived mindset of the individual while attending school. Even though the researcher of this project cannot select the students, the research can develop study questions and writing assignments to facilitate and stipulate the importance of this research. The research can determine what quantitative analysis is used to offer clarification of the problems facing incarcerated individuals, but not the focus of this research. The number of participants is limited to individuals enrolled in the HiSET or GED classes, and participation is voluntary. The location and time of the questionnaire, interviews, and focus group is at the discretion of the prison administrators, but the county is offering full cooperation in meeting the needs for this study.

As to the bias of the researcher, there is one. Having taught classes in the prison system since 2006 and in classes at the collegiate level since 2002, I have seen the despair of the incarcerated individuals, but I have also seen the hope and desire for change. I have also seen the inadequacies of the penal system and the educational programs, but I have also seen programs that have had a positive influence on the lives of many individuals. In this study, this researcher must avoid preconceived attitudes and emotions and deliver results that were determined to be unbiased and accurate as to the perception of public education and the influence on criminal activity.

Theoretical Underpinnings

The theoretical underpinnings and effectiveness of this research are based on the experiences of interactions of the researcher interacting with incarcerated individuals. The research must have an atmosphere of trust with the goal to assist the incarcerated individual to develop a sense of purpose guided by values. To fully understand the mindset of the incarcerated individual is another research study, but it is important for this research for the researcher to have a basic understanding. Individuals entering prison have a strong feeling of despair, loneliness, guilt, and lack of self-worth. They lack a vision of purpose in life and are centered on survival. This knowledge comes from the researcher's experience teaching and counseling inmates. The purpose of this study was to find if public education experiences influenced criminal activity. To understand the positive or negative outcomes, the theories of Carl Rogers have been incorporated into this research project. Rogers stipulates in his article "The Necessary and Sufficient Conditions of Therapeutic Personality Change," that an individual must have ownership in the process, or change in attitude will not happen (p. 8).

It is important that the researcher gain trust and respect with the participants by making them feel included in the research by having them play an important role in developing awareness and importance of public school education rather than "viewing people as inherently flawed, with problematic behaviors and thoughts that require treatment, person-centered therapy identifies that each person has the capacity and desire for personal growth and change" (Raskin, 141–186). The researcher must develop a relationship of trust and empathy with the participants for them to feel that they a part of a project that could potentially have a positive impact. The foundation of initiating change must utilize motivational theories of learning. Fundamental sources are Allan Wigfield and Jacquelynne S. Eccles articles "Expectancy-Value Theory of Achievement Motivation" and "Motivational Beliefs, Values, and Goals" (p. 68).

To achieve success, one must first address the present organizational structure and offer a solution to developing a better learning environment, not only for the students but also for instructors and administrators. The stark reality is that prison is not a nice place. It is a cold, hard place with razor-wire fences, steel doors, and usually eight-by-six cells with two steel beds, a sink, and a toilet. Inmates are told when to go to bed and when to get up, what they can eat, and when they can talk. They must seek permission to open doors. The inmates are told what they can do, what classes they can attend, and what courses they must take. An environment such as this is designed in a way that tends to prioritize behavior and procedures with an emphasis to simply follow orders. This mentality diminishes the thought process, and critical thinking is not encouraged.

An underpinning theory from this research could be the environmental conditions and the value of self-worth, self-esteem, and self-actualization of accomplishment. Denise A Kensit states that, according to Rogers,

Individuals have within themselves vast resources for self-understanding and for altering their self-concepts, basic attitudes, and self-directed behavior; these resources can be tapped if a definable climate of facilitative psychological attitudes can be provided. (pp. 345–351)

Once these theories are incorporated into this research, the foundation will be established to offer validation and credibility to this research project.

Summary

In summary, the problems are extensive ranging from society's lack of acceptance of rehabilitation to the legislative denial of a course of action for rehabilitation over penance and the correctional institutions inability to properly educate and advocate for educational reform. The purpose of this study focuses on the education experiences in the public school system to see if there was a correlation between inmate's perspectives and the influence education had on criminal activity. The study also focuses on changing the mindset of the incarcerated individual from despair, loneliness, and isolation to one of self-worth by participating a research project that could have a positive impact on initiating change in our present public educational system, as well as changing the mindset of penance to rehabilitation in our criminal justice facilities.

CHAPTER 2

Literature Review

The purpose of this study is to examine the effects of public education and the influence it had on criminal activities of incarcerated women inmates in the county Sheriff's Office jail facilities and paroled men from the Department of Corrections. There is abundance of literature addressing inmates' educational experience while being incarcerated, which was addressed to establish a relationship between education, recidivism, and criminal activity. In this chapter, the focus was on the incarcerated individual's educational mindset in relation to public education and to address under-representation of the inmate's public school experience in literature. The chapter included theories of mindsets and cause of criminal behavior based on social, cultural, economic perceptions related to behavior. The theories of ethics and self-efficacy are mentioned to establish a relation between criminal behavior and the past mindset and were used to alter the criminal mindset to become a positive member of society.

This research project focuses on the past educational reflections that inmates had in their public education experiences and if there was a correlation with criminal activity. To comprehend the relationship between the educational mindset while attending school and criminal activity, an extensive literature review must be incorporated to fully understand the role of education in the mindset individual and offer solutions to the potential of what can be achieved with the inclusion of rehabilitative educational programs. Some of the literature is based on recidivism, postrelease employment, and the relationship between correctional education and academic performance in the public school system.

Literature has been incorporated throughout the first chapter with the intent to offer a broad spectrum of knowledge showing the problems that face the incarcerated individuals, but also some of the educational programs in correctional facilities. The broad-based literature review was narrowed to offer concepts that will be beneficial to understanding the problems and possible solutions. By understanding where we have been in our educational philosophy and analyzing the effectiveness, we can be proactive and initiate new programs that will be beneficial to all concerned. By developing a base of knowledge of the problems facing, not only the incarcerated individual but society in general, and by presenting a historical foundation of the problems relating the lack of, or the improper forms of instruction, an awareness can be initiated to develop a solution. Equity audits were conducted to further understand the societal problems facing the incarcerated individual and to establish guidelines for educational accountability and equity. The source for the audits came from *Using Equity Audit to Create Equitable and Excellent Schools* by Linda Skrla, Kathryn Bell McKenzie, and James Joseph Scheurich (2009).

Instructional Learning

Marsha Rossiter argues in the article "Possible Selves: An Adult Education Perspective" that learning "the concept of possible selves as a concept more closely related to the felt identity of persons. Possible selves refer to the future oriented components of the self-concept" (Rossiter 2007, 5). Albert Bandura explains in *Self-Efficacy: The Exercise of Control* the importance of learning in that "students' self-efficacy beliefs influence their performance in several ways. It is a consistent predictor of their pursued course of action, coping behaviors (i.e., effort, persistence, and resilience), and ultimately, their achievements" (1997, 43). According to Bandura, learning is a four-step process of attention, retention, production, and motivation (1997, 89). The attention process is the functionality or value of instruction. The retention process is the cognitive capabilities to further retain the functional value of educational learning. The production process allows for a course of action, and the motivational process is the self-efficacy or self-actuation that the individual has value and a purpose.

Four Step Process

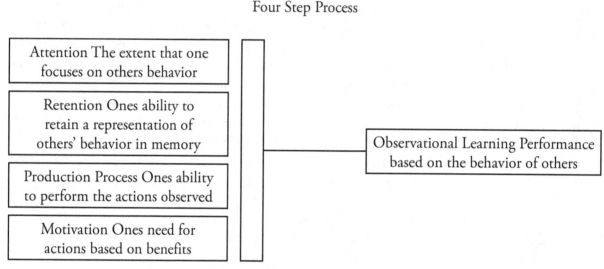

Figure 1. Observational Learning

The understanding of Bandura's theory on behavior change is vital to this study. Figure 2 shows the process of learning and how an individual's past experiences, the influence of peer behavior, social pressure, and the emotional state of the individual can determine the outcome of one's behavior (p. 195).

Efficacy Expectations

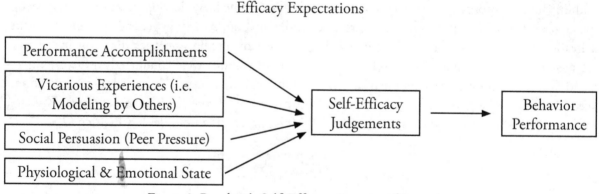

Figure 2. Bandura's Self-Efficacy Process of Learning

According to Frank Pajares in his paper "Gender and Perceived Self-Efficacy in Self-Regulated Learning," the beliefs students develop about their academic capabilities help determine what they do with the knowledge and skills they have learned: "Consequently, their academic performances are, in part, the result of what they come to believe they have accomplished and can accomplish" (p. 116). Bandura further supports Pajares's self-efficacy concept by defining *self-efficacy* as

> the individual's perceived ability to succeed at or accomplish certain tasks. Academic self-efficacy is thus central to success in school or education and can serve as an explanatory factor for why people's achievement may differ even though they have similar knowledge and skills. (p. 107)

Self-efficacy or self-actuation is the motivating factor of finding benefits or rewards for accomplishments of obtaining a sense of value and purpose.

The Economic Value of Social and Emotional Learning, as written by Clive Belfield, Brooks Bowden, Alli Klapp, Henry Levin, Robert Shand, and Sabine Zander, offers a format to enhance Bandura's and Pajares's concept on behavior change (2015). Before effective programs can be implemented, a six-step format must be initiated by providing social and emotional learning interventions as guidelines for positive interactions.

Table 1. Descriptions of the Six Social and Emotional Learning Interventions

Intervention	Grades and Student Groups
4R's—Reading, Writing, Respect, and Resolution Learning and literacy programs to combat aggression and violence	Grades K-5 Disadvantaged
Positive Action—A school based curriculum designed to promote students positive thinking, actions, and self-concept	Grades 3-8 All
Life Skill Training—Classroom intervention to reduce substance abuse and violence	Grades 6-12 At-risk students
Second Step—Social skills curriculum to improve problem-solving and emotional management	Grades PK-10 Disadvantaged
Responsive Classroom—Improve teacher efficacy to influence social and emotion (SE) skills and school community	Grades 3-5 All
Social and Emotional Training (Sweden)—Classroom intervention to support cognitive and SE competencies	Grades 1-9 All

The first phase is to develop learning and literacy programs to confront aggression and violent behavior. The usage of reading, writing, respect, and resolution curriculum focuses on the social and emotional learning and literary development by developing themes that relate to the resolution of conflict, the appreciation of diversity, and the importance of interpersonal relationships (p. 21). The second step is to develop positive actions through a curriculum that is designed to develop positive thinking, actions, and behavior choices. "This intervention is intended to increase intrinsic motivation to learn and reinforce positive behavior" (p. 30). The third step was designed to develop life skills by reducing substance abuse and violence by teaching social and emotional skills to build self-confidence and self-esteem, thus developing life skills to resist peer pressure and to limit the level of anxiety that is a contributing factor in health-related matters. It is divided into three categories of knowledge and skills to resist the usage of alcohol, tobacco, and other drugs; personal management skills; and social skills to build assertiveness and self-confidence (pp. 30–31).

The fourth step, ironically titled the "second step" encourages critical-thinking skills by integrating cognitive behavior models that relate to problem solving and emotional management. It is designed to emphasize empathy of others as an approach to understand themselves and to improve communication skills that reduces aggressive and delinquent behavior (p. 34). The fifth step focuses on the teacher interaction with their students, as well as the design of subject matter to develop a responsive classroom. The importance of this step is that the focus is on teacher development to improve their "self-efficacy," so they can have a greater impact on the students to enhance their own "self-efficacy." By doing so, the purpose is to positive "social, emotional, academic and non-academic outcomes and to build a strong school community" (p. 37). The sixth step was modeled after a Swedish program that evaluated methods of social and emotional training (SET). The program is a classroom-based intervention designed to "support students' cognitive and social and emotional competencies" (p. 40).

The Swedish program show positive effects for emotional and social outcomes. The importance of this study that was written for Collaborative for Academic, Social, and Emotional Learning (CASEL) was that it included the cost and benefits of initiating this program into a school environment. The school theory of action framework was developed by CASEL to further enhance the effectiveness of the educational experience. The concept emphasizes the training of teachers and administrators and welcomes parents as partners so they can become part of the solution and take ownership in the development of the school experience. It also focuses on relationships between student to student, teacher or adult to student, and adult to adult. By doing so, a coalition of collaborative support defines the role of education, not just administrators. The six phases of developing an effective and supportive learning environment are part of the social and emotional learning (SEL) format (2018).

1) Develop a vision that prioritizes academic, social, and emotional learning.
2) Conduct SEL-related resources and needs assessment to inform goals for school-wide SEL implementation.
3) Design and implement effective professional learning programs to build internal capacity for academic, social, and emotional learning.
4) Adopt and implement evidence-based programs for academic, social, and emotional learning across all grades.
5) Integrate SEL at all three levels of school functioning.
6) Curriculum and instruction.
7) School-wide practices and policies.
8) Family and community partnership.
9) Establish a process to continuously improve academic, social, and emotional learning through inquiry and data collection.

These principles are significant and can have a tremendous impact on the development of more effective learning environments, which directly effects not only the students but also the teachers, administrators, family, and the community. In order to implement these principles of social and emotional learning (SEL), effective leadership is required to guide these concepts into action. Doulas Reeves, in his book *From Leading to Succeeding: The Seven Elements of Effective Leadership in Education*, offers a leadership approach that can directly enhance the SEL programs and offer guidance for the implementation of effective programs (2016). The implementation of an effective educational program is the responsibility of the administration but must be a coalition of support from all segments of the educational environment, including parents and community. The word that Reeves uses as a guide is *passion*. The administrators must have a passion for continuous learning and developing meaningful outcomes. The seven leadership elements that should be used in the SEL educational format are the following:

1) *Purpose*. Administrators must have a clear and concise vision with a mission statement that is also clear and concise. The purpose must be a collaborative effort to engage as many segments society to develop a strategy of effectiveness and ownership.

2) *Trust*. "Leaders can be forgiven for many mistakes as long as their colleagues trust them" This is a quote from the beginning of chapter 2 entitled "Trust" (p. 23). Trust is built on many factors, including developing a coalition of collaborative participation, so the whole system takes ownership. The statement of purpose must be followed through, or if changed, an explanation must be given as to the reason why. Reeves states that mistakes happen, and the trust factor is determined on how a leader resolves the situation. Leaders must be able to walk the walk and not just talk the talk.

3) *Focus*. Conscious leaders have choices on what they will do or will not do (p. 31). Reeves uses the term *calendar integrity* to help visualize the importance of their values and priorities. The focus must be on their purpose, mission, and vision of collaborative strategies. Reeves mentioned that focused leaders are "boring, fragmented leaders show enthusiasm that gains popularity without impact" (p. 31). Focused leaders require accountability, which substantiates and validates the sense of purpose and sustainable school improvement of continuous leaning. Focused leaders tend to accomplish tasks and be able to address other issues. This gives the focused leader leverage for accomplishing more important tasks, and being boring is less important than being respected for getting things done.

4) *Leverage*. By accomplishing goals and tasks, one gains an advantage by being focused and trusted to fulfill a responsibility. Leverage is gained by developing a trust with fellow cohorts that ethical standards are applied. Being focused on task-orientated projects and completion of the mission gains a leverage for the next situation of importance. As an administrative leader, the focus must be on curriculum improvement, professional development, and on the well-being of the students. This focus gives the leader leverage to continue the renewal of quality teaching.

5) *Feedback*. The leverage one gains can be quickly lost if informative feedback is not given in a proper timeframe or format. Hattie and Yates, in their book *Visible Learning and the Science of How We Learn*, identify feedback as "one of the most powerful factors implicated in academic learning and resultant achievement" (2014, 68). Giving proper and timely feedback reinforces that their purpose is fulfilled and that the administrator can be trusted because of being focused on the subject. Proper feedback help facilitate the "art of leading change" (p. 6).

6) *Change*. The change element is what is needed to ensure continuous learning and productive school system. But change is not an easy task to accomplish if the basic elements of effective leadership are not adhered to. Reeves established the guidelines by demanding the elements of purpose, trust, focus, leverage, feedback so that change can be a positive experience. An experience that can lead to sustainability.

7) *Sustainability*. The importance of sustainability is that they endure. According to John P. Kotter, in his book *Leading Change*, is to anchor the sustainability process and new approaches into the culture of the organization (Kotter, p. 23). The six preceding elements of *From Leading to Succeeding* will be needed to successfully initiate programs for continuous improvement in an educational system. The sustainability of new programs will be adhered to if the leadership adheres to these elements.

The previously mention theories and concepts are fundamental to this research as they give guidance and credibility for the evaluation of existing conditions and the possible implementation of new programs and curriculums. The benefit of SEL and action-based theory is for all students, whether they are in prison or an education system. These theories and concepts must include a motivational factor by developing a sense of purpose and understanding the *why*.

Motivation

The incarcerated adult learner has several motivating factors or reasons for taking educational classes. The adult incarcerated learner is motivated for self-improvement to obtain a better lifestyle with greater income potential to support themselves and their families. This is a difficult task, as studies have proven. The jail or prison system is to educate the individual so they can get a job and hopefully not return to prison. According to John Nally, Susan Lockwood, Taiping Ho, and Katie Knutson in their 2014 article, "Post-Release Recidivism and Employment Among Different Types of Released Offenders: A 5-year Follow-Up Study in the United States":

> Participation in education during incarceration can play an important role in the daily life of many prisoners and has significant consequences for resettlement on release. The main focus of this 5-year (2005–2009) follow-up study of released offenders was to explore the post-release employment and recidivism among different types of released offenders before, during, and after the economic recession of 2008. The dataset of this study contained a cohort of 6,561 offenders who were released from the Indiana Department of Correction (IDOC), United States, throughout 2005. Results of this study revealed 37.0 percent of violent offenders, 38.2 percent of non-violent offenders, 36.3 percent of sex offenders, and 36.9 percent of drug offenders were never employed since release from prison. The recidivism rate was 46.6 percent among violent offenders, 48.6 percent among non-violent offenders, 54.7 percent among sex offenders, and 45.8 percent among drug offenders, respectively. Most importantly, the results of this study revealed that an offender's education and post-release employment were significantly and statistically correlated with recidivism, regardless of the offender's classification. This study also found a relatively high unemployment rate among released offenders within the first year of release from prison. Accordingly, almost half of the recidivist offenders were re-incarcerated within 12 months of the initial release. (pp. 16–34).

The goal is for the incarcerated individual to be self-motivated to pursue a better lifestyle and become productive members of society during incarceration and after being released. The study indicated a level of recidivism that shows approximately 50 percent return to prison for various reasons within a year, and these statistics are like other studies on recidivism (Cooper 2014, 1–31). Once an inmate is released, the mindset is that they can achieve success and not return to prison. The motivational factors are self-centered that they have the training to succeed, but there are more difficulties and originally perceived. The mindset changes from one of hope to one of despair. The foundation of initiating change must utilize motivational theories of learning. Fundamental sources are Allan Wigfield and Jacquelynne S. Eccles in the articles "Expectancy-Value Theory of Achievement Motivation" and "Motivational Beliefs, Values, and Goals" (p. 68). To achieve success, one must first address the present organizational structure and offer a solution to developing a better learning environment not only for the students but also for the instructors.

The expectancy-value theory was used to develop a coalition of collaborative support. By understanding the present format of the county educational programing and the initiatives being established and talked about, motivational theories are already being applied. The theories on reason for engagement dealing with competence, expectancy, beliefs, goals, values are important tools in developing new enhanced learning centers. The question that still must be answered is *why*, not only for the instructors but mainly for the students. The instructors must present intrinsic motivation by developing enjoyment and creating a sense of purpose. The extrinsic motivation of getting a reward is secondary and important to achieve recognition not only for themselves but also for the family to be aware of the accomplishment. By incorporating intrinsic motivational techniques into the classroom, students will begin to develop self-determination skills by utilizing the theory that humans are motivated by stimulation and achieving competence.

Csikszentmihalyi (1990) defined *intrinsic motivation* as totally engaged in an activity and labeled his theory as the "Flow." Individuals are emotionally engaged in an activity, almost a Martin Buber "I–Thou" or "I–It moment of interaction (Patton, 73); the question remains *why*. One knows "what" happened and "how" it happened, but maybe not the why. This must be further explored to understand the thought process or mindset to change to another possible course of action by establishing goals. Dale Schunk, in his book *Learning Theories as Educational Perspective*, writes about the importance of goals in in promoting self-efficiency and improved performance by reflecting on one's purpose (p. 135). Purpose is guided by values. The expectancy-value theory articulated by Eccles and Wigfield stipulates that there are values related to choices that have a cost to determine course of action or options. Students who can find attainment value, intrinsic value, utility value, and understanding the cost will attain the personal value of accomplishment and find self-worth. The emphasis of the self-worth theory is vitally important for the students to understand and appreciate. By establishing a positive self-image of self-worth, students are more apt to get out of their pseudo-safety zone and try new endeavors.

Daniel Willingham, in his book *Why Don't Students Like School?* emphasizes the relationship between environment and memory. He concludes that educators "must ensure that students acquire background knowledge parallel with practical critical thinking skills" (p. 29). Social scientists must be cognizant of the environment from which the participant came from and utilize positive motivational skills to initiate change by developing purpose guided by values. By understanding environmental conditions and the importance of motivational theories, potential outcomes could have a positive impact on not just changing one person's life but to changing a system from penance to rehabilitation. Daniel Pink, in his book *Drive*, offers an insight as to why individuals need to take charge of their own lives and offers a guideline to motivate oneself. He defines the need for self-motivation and also gives a structure to facilitate change by emphasizing three basic elements: *autonomy*, *mastery*, and *purpose* (pp. 83–145). These principles will be valuable in developing solutions to the problem of lack of motivation not only for the student but also for the instructor.

Mindset

The motivating mindset factors are that the individual has been court-ordered to participate in classes or to indicate to the parole board that they are attempting to reeducate themselves. Knowing the past and present mindset of the incarcerated individual is vital to the importance of this study to offer solutions for positive rehabilitation back into society. The mindset of the incarcerated individual must change from self-centered to family-centered. In an article written for the Texas Department of Corrections by E. Mosley titled "Incarcerated—Children of Parents in Prison Impacted," it reports that 70 percent of the children of incarcerated parents will also be incarcerated (2008, 1). With this disturbing fact, the purpose of continuing education is not just for the individual but to become a role model for their children by developing a sense of urgency and importance to a purpose- and value-driven educational experience. Through *self-efficacy* and *self-actualization*, the purpose or mindset can change. Their purpose is no longer self-centered but child-centered. They need to develop a sense of purpose guided by values to change their behavior is the motivating factor to achieve the positive outcome and goal they desire. This can be facilitated by correction instructors and officers.

The mindset and motivation of prison practitioners is another contributing factor to the success or decline of the incarcerated individual. While it is clear the motivation and mindset influence learning experiences within the facility, it is the nature of educational programs within the prison system that must be addressed. Carol Dweck's book *Mindset: The New Psychology of Success* develops an insight as to the thought process of individuals, especially teachers and parents by offering concepts on how to initiate change (p. 177). Further procedural expectations are to develop and understanding the nature of the narrative stories and initiate conversations for solutions to the problems. Incorporating Simon Sinek Golden Circle concept from his book *Start with Why: How Great Leaders Inspire Everyone to Take Action*, students will begin to self-motivate to answer the questions: Why am I doing this? What is my purpose? How am I going to get there? The traditional methodology for the Golden Circle is the work from the inside and ask the questions why, how, and what? For this study, I also want to start with the question, What happened? Then I ask how it happened and, finally, *why* this happened.

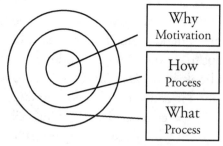

Figure 3. Golden Circle

The facilitation of the Golden Circle must have a foundation built on Maslow's Hierarchy of Needs. In an article written for *Psychological Review* in 1943, "A Theory of Human Motivation," Maslow articulates the importance of motivation sequences to achieve self-actualization (pp. 370–396). The primary stage in developing cognitive motivation is physiological. One must first be cognizant of the basic needs of shelter, food, water, etc. By taking care of the basic needs, one can move to the next stage, making sure the student has the confidence that there is safety and security. This is important because of negative peer pressure from previous involvement with gangs or even the home environment. The third stage of development is making sure the student feels he or she is not alone and that they have a support group that will assist them through difficult times by offering guidance and encouragement. With these stages in place, one's self esteem and sense of value has increased to the degree that the final stage of self-actualization will be completed.

Martin and Joomis (2007) adds an addition stage of aesthetic value to the hierarchy of needs (p. 72–75). Creativity and the confidence to express oneself is the additional stage that allows an individual to be able to identify with self-expression and give value to their purpose. The other stage added is the need to know. The first four stages are referred to as *deficiency* stages, and the top three are *growth*. Before achieving self-actualization, the first four stages must be addressed to motivate the student to obtain their goals. Maslow's Hierarchy of Needs is a fundamental tool to assist the inmate-students develop a sense of accomplishment and self-worth. Even though we cannot fully concentrate on the physiological needs of the students—such as food, shelter, clothing, etc.—we can make the atmosphere within the classroom setting a safe place where the students can escape the rigorous and impersonal settings of the prison cell. We can also initiate social needs by establishing a sense of belonging to a group that will have an impact on initiating change in the educational system. By doing so, self-esteem is being developed to the realization that "I can make a difference," which leads to self-actualization of *growth needs* and accomplishments.

The Process of Self-Actualization

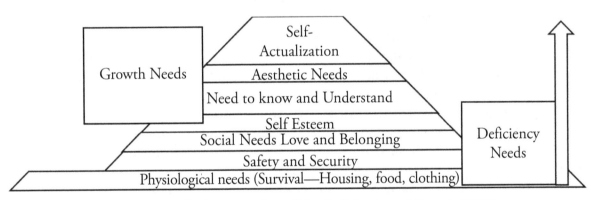

Figure 4. Maslow's Hierarchy of Needs (Martin and Joomis 2007)

Institutional Educational Programs

Margo DelliCarpini argues that through educational instruction and programing, the recidivism rate is reduced. In her article "Building a Better Life: Implementing a Career and Technical Education Program for Incarcerate Youth," she reports that there is a positive effect in terms of program completion and vocational training (p. 283). Lois M. Davis, senior policy researcher at the Rand Corporation, stipulates that here is strong evidence that correctional education plays a key role in reducing recidivism. The article entitled "Education and Vocational Training in Prisons Reduces Recidivism, Improves Job Outlook" stresses the importance of education, but more research is needed to determine which courses are effective (p. 1–3). Davis also reports in *Evaluating the Effectiveness of Correctional Education* that effective classroom instruction reduces the risk of recidivism by 13 percent (2013, 33).

By studying and introducing these articles, new enhancements can be added to the educational programing of the jail facilities and change the mindset from penance to rehabilitation. This study of past educational experiences will also provide an understanding for future enhancements to the program. Most academic articles of inmates' perception of educational experiences have been related to jail or prison educational programs and not public school perceptions. The emphasis has been on correcting educational programming in the prison with the knowledge of what has occurred and how it is being done, but not answering the question of *why* the education has failed.

An article was published in the Conservative Daily Post on November 17, 2017, written by April Horning entitled "Democrat-Run Baltimore Schools Sink to 13 Year Low as City Crime Increases Drastically" that further emphasizes the importance of education instruction and motivation. The intent of the article was to show the correlation between public education and criminal activities. The article stipulates the absentee rate of over 25 percent and discusses some of the reasons and perceptions of student attitudes but does not offer a solution.

Michelle Moeller, Scott L. Day, Beverly D. Rivera, in their article "How Is Education Perceived on the Inside? A Preliminary Study of Adult Males in a Correctional Setting," published in the *Journal of Correctional Education*, stipulate that educational courses can help reduce the rate of recidivism and increase student attitudes towards the importance of education (2004, 40–59). The article also indicates that educational programs can serve as a tool to be used in parole hearings, and the classes are functional for that purpose—that is a general opinion of the students. Karen Miner-Romanoff wrote in the *American Journal of Criminal Justice* her article "Student Perceptions of Juvenile Offender Accounts in Criminal Justice Education," where she describes having upper-level college students view a video of juvenile offenders recounting their experiences of being institutionalized and fears upon release (2014, 611–629). The article answers the basic questions of what and how it happened, but not the *why*. It was a quantitative study with one qualitative question that revealed the impact of the inmates' attitudes of the juvenile educational courses. According to the Rand Corporation report on meta-analysis, most of correctional facilities have certified instructors, volunteers, interns, and use a variety of computer programs to facilitate the educational needs (Davis 2013, 37).

The utilization of college professors, volunteers, and interns helps offset the cost reduction in educational expenditures. Traditional classroom instruction is used in lecture format, rote memorization, face-to-face assistance, peer tutoring, and some team teaching. The difficulty is the lack of collaboration on subject matter due to different educational programs. Some facilities have computer access to the traditional programs, such as PLATO and the Advanced Instructional Management System (AIMS), which allowed the students to independently study the courses they needed at their own pace. The classrooms were staffed by facility employees, interns, or peer tutors to handle technical difficulties. The AutoSkills—Component Reading Subskills Program—which was reportedly designed to teach cognitive subskills of reading and instruction, was conducted by literacy teachers (Davis 2013, 49). While other classrooms did not have access to computers and had to use lecture format and HiSET textbooks.

The difficulty in teaching in a classroom setting is the differentiation of grade equivalency or the academic achievement gap between inmate students. The Florida Department of Corrections states in their 2011 annual report that 71.7 percent of incarcerated individuals test at a sixth grade or below GED preparation level. Table 2 below groups the grade levels of the inmates admitted during FY 2009–10 into three different categories: basic literacy, functional literacy, and GED prep skills.

Table 2. Florida Department of Corrections Literacy Analysis
Tested Literacy Skill Levels at Admission (First Tests of Adult Basic Education [TABE])

Literacy Level	White Males	White Females	Black Males	Black Females	Other Males	Other Females	Total	Percent	Cumulative
Basic Literacy (1.0-5.9)	5,021	616	8,805	636	518	30	15,626	46.3%	46.3%
Functional Literacy (6.0-8.9)	3,811	701	3,439	360	220	20	8,551	25.4%	71.7%
GED Prep (9.0-12.0)	5.563	1,285	2,167	281	234	24	9,554	28.3%	100%
Data Unavailable	2,552	133	1,142	83	338	13	3,261		
Total	15,947	2,735	15,553	1,360	1,310	87	36,992	100%	100%
Median	7.4	8.6	5.4	6.0	5.7	6.4	6.2		

The literacy analysis clearly indicates the severity of the problem as it relates to the success of the individual being released back into society. It also shows the level of competency that the present educational system has on incarcerated individual. Even though the United States is a multicultural society that initiates different concerns about education, there are other countries that have programs that have succeeded in initiating educational programs that have benefited the released individual.

International Perspective

There have been several dissertations and articles written about education in prison facilities, and Michelle Pettit's doctoral dissertation entitled *Exemplary Educational Programs in Norwegian Prisons: A Case Study of Norwegian Attitudes and Humanitarian Practices* (2012) stipulates that the process of success is based on qualified educators that motivate inmate students to the importance of education in developing a career. Pettit also wrote an article, "The Educational Service in Swedish Prisons: Successful programs of Academic and Vocational Training," that reenforces the principles of meaningful vocational training leading to successful reintegration into society. The importance of these articles is that they offer a solution to the problem, whereas most of the articles offer a perspective of the educational classes conducted in prison or the jail facilities (2012).

Michelle Brown wrote in 2009 *The Culture of Punishment: Prison, Society, and Spectacle*, published by New York University Press, the perceptions of the public on incarcerated individuals, but not on the inmate's perception. The article was an interesting perspective explaining that the public is generally more distant from the practice of punishment, and they tend to be harsher in their judgments and encourage punishment over rehabilitation. Research articles are limited to the inmate's perception of their public school experiences, but not limited to their attitudes to the educational programs while being incarcerated. One of the major difficulties for a released individual is the acceptance by society.

As stated in chapter 1, the original intent of the correctional system was a program of penance to reflect on behavior patterns and obtain grace through religious study and meditation (Schmid, 553). By offering different correction systems to contrast, one will be able to compare the different approaches to the function of prison and rehabilitation. In Norway, the correctional philosophy is to develop curriculum that will develop life skills that will enhance a positive return to society. Per Michele Pettit, the process is based on qualified educators that motivate the students to the importance of education in developing a career (2012). Pettit stipulates that the Swedish prison academic and vocational programs are based on the "principle of returning the inmates to normalcy by teaching meaningful work that can lead to successful re-integration back into society" (2012). By comparing the different philosophies of incarceration from penance to rehabilitation, we will be able to offer solutions to the present needs of the US correctional education programs. Researching present educational programs in the US prison system and foreign countries allows for comparison of the effectiveness of rehabilitation and should instill a mind shift from penance to rehabilitation as a social priority.

Societal Perspective

The social cognitive theory is explained by Bandura in his book *Social Foundation of Thought and Action* (1986) and stipulates that human behavior is influenced by the environment and personal factors of self-efficacy. The environmental factors are extremely cognizant to this research in that the influence of the family, community, and peer associations are factors in behavioral patterns, whereas the personal factors include personal beliefs or instincts that develop motivational responses.

Behavioral Factors

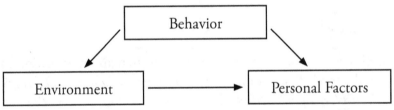

Figure 5. Bandura's social Cognitive Theory Model

Bandura further explains that those motivational responses are influenced by rewards, and if there is no incentive, then action does not occur. The incentive or rewards for this study are the positive or negative interactions with family, peers, community, and schooling. The important aspect of this Social Cognitive Theory for this research is of norms or expectations that are required to survive in a particular community. Those norms control behavior. In an article, "Theory of Behavior Change," written for Communication for Governance and Accountability Program (CommGap, an affiliate of the World Bank), the authors further clarify Bandura's position by the inclusion of six basic principles that apply to this research. The authors cite C. L. Perry's article "How Outcome Expectations—The Personal Judgment of the likely Consequences and the Importance of those Expectations."

Individuals, Environments, and Health Behavior Interact: Social Learning Theory (1990,3).

1) *Self-efficacy.* The personal judgment to perform a certain behavior.
2) *Outcome expectations.* A judgment of the likely consequences of behavior will produce the importance of expectations that may also drive behavior.

3) *Self-control.* The ability to control behavior.
4) *Reinforcement.* A condition that increases or decreases the likelihood a behavior will continue.
5) *Emotional coping.* The ability to handle an emotional stimulus.
6) *Observational learning.* The acquisition of behaviors by observing actions and outcomes of others.

These six elements offer an insight as to the mindset of the incarcerated individual and the impact society, especially peers, have on their behavior. They relate to the cost and reward of deciding a course of action. In this study, the participants indicate a mode of survival as the reward and the cost becomes secondary. Through observation, the individual learns to remove barriers that hinder activation of a behavior and learns to cope with the decision. This mindset is also reinforced by the cost/reward ratio experience of previous behavioral patterns, and decisions are controlled to justify the means to an end or expected outcomes. The self-efficacy or personal judgment to perform was established using the criteria "the five remain elements." William Huitt and Courtney Dawson wrote about the importance of motivation in *Social Development: Why It Is Important and How To Impact It* (2011). Huitt and Dawson used the CASEL (Collaborative for Academic, Social, and Emotional Learning) as a model to initiate change and identified five competencies that provide a foundation for personal growth (2011, 2).

1) *Self-awareness*: knowing what one is feeling and thinking; having a realistic assessment of one's own abilities and a well-grounded sense of self-confidence.
2) *Social awareness*: understanding what others are feeling and thinking; appreciating and interacting positively with diverse groups.
3) *Self-management*: handling one's emotions so they facilitate rather than interfere with task achievement; setting and accomplishing goals; persevering in the face of setbacks and frustrations.
4) *Relationship skills*: establishing and maintaining healthy and rewarding relationships based on clear communication, cooperation, resistance to inappropriate social pressure, negotiating solutions to conflict, and seeking help when needed.
5) *Responsible decision-making*: making choices based on an accurate consideration of all relevant factors and the likely consequences of alternative courses of action, respecting others, and taking responsibility for one's decisions.

The importance of understanding these competencies is that they offer a possible clarification as to why incarcerated individuals have failed in school and in socially accepted behavior. Besides understanding the negative mindset of the individual, the competencies offer a possible solution to initiate change.

Societal Priorities

The instruction in state and county jails is based on the funding available and the resources from the community and is a key factor in the success of the programs. The difficulty is that funding is the key factor in developing educational programs. August 6, 2017, the Associated Press announced that past Governor Eric Greitens of Missouri once "advocated increasing education and job training programs for inmates, he signed a budget that cut $1.4 million from Missouri Department of Corrections rehabilitation programs, with most of the reduction coming in education programs." In the February 2014 RAND report "How Effective is Correctional Education, and Where Do We Go from Here?" Lois Davis found that academic courses were hardest hit by the state funding cuts:

> There has been a dramatic contraction of the prison education system, particularly those programs focused on academic instruction versus vocational training. There are now fewer teachers, course offerings and fewer students enrolled in academic education programs.

The effect of the staffing and capacity cost-cutting measures on teachers for academic programs were particularly felt in medium-sized and large states. Overall, there was, on average, a 4 percent decrease in the number of academic teachers who were employees. The largest decrease occurred in medium-sized and large states (on average, 44 percent and 20 percent, respectively, compared with a 5 percent decrease for small states (Davis 2014, 19–21).

Emphasizing the importance of rehabilitative education and clarifying the cost factor to the taxpayer of incarceration due to the influence of the public K-12 educational experience could benefit the mind shift from penance to rehabilitation as a method to cure the rising cost of incarceration. Another societal priority is the diminishing the academic achievement gap between inner-city and suburban schools. Tony Wagner stipulates in his book *The Global Achievement Gap* that the school systems need to incorporate seven fundamental survival skills that would develop a more functional and purposeful educational experience (pp. 14–42).

1) Critical thinking and problem-solving—the ability to ask good questions
2) Collaborative across networks and leading by influence
3) Agility and adaptability
4) Initiative and entrepreneurialism
5) Effective oral and written communication
6) Accessing and analyzing information
7) Curiosity and imagination

The seven survival skills are incorporated to offer potential solutions in changing the mindset of educators and develop excitement among the students. Anthony Muhammad writes in his book *Overcoming the Achievement Gap Trap* that this gap is becoming a lower priority and that "private citizens are being convinced that the achievement gap is caused by some inherent flaw in the students (victim), not a systemic problem that could be fixed by improving professional practice" (2015, xvii). Wagner's and Muhammad's solutions are practical and have been applied in chapter 5 as part of the solution.

Societal Influences

The question still remains *why*. Is there an implicit bias as to the educational needs of culturally diverse schools? Do these biases have a direct link to the research question of an inquiry of an inmate's perception of public school education and criminal activity? These questions were asked of the students participating in this research project, and the findings are recorded in the next chapter.

The foundation for this particular inquiry is racial relations and the impact on criminal activity. In an article written by Peggy McIntosh, "White Privilege: Unpacking the Invisible Knapsack," she writes that "men work from a base of unacknowledged privilege, I understood that much of their oppressiveness was unconscious" (p.1). McIntosh also states that "frequent charges from women of color that white women whom they encounter are oppressive." If this is the attitude, this researcher wanted to ask the student-inmates if this was a factor in their criminal behavior. A classroom session was conducted to address this "white privilege" scenario and to offer clarification as to the impact on their behavior. Included in this discussion were aspects of racial and ethnic relations.

McIntosh's article was interesting as it initiated conversation and relevance to the past and present educational experiences. The question of implicit bias was addressed, and solutions were discussed. The base for these discussions was from an article written by Shane Safir for the George Lucas Foundation, "5 Keys to Challenging Implicit Bias" (March 11, 2016). The importance of this article is that it explains implicit biases "often stand in opposition to a person's stated beliefs" (pp.1–2).

1) *Disproportionality in discipline.* "Policies that appear racially neutral on their face but result in the over-representation of students of color—particularly black boys—in suspensions, expulsions, and referrals for subjected infractions like defiance."

2) *Disproportionality in special education.* "Misguided placements that result in the over-representation of culturally and linguistically diverse students in special education programs."

3) *Teacher mindset and beliefs.* "Underestimating the intellectual capacity of culturally and linguistically diverse students and often girls inside the classroom."

4) *Tracking.* "School policies that automatically place students of color in remedial or low-tracked courses."

5) *Dominant discourse.* "Ways of thinking and talking about students and families that diminish, underestimate, or even pathologize them."

Safir offers solutions to this preconceived bias as a form of rehabilitation, not only in the public education mindset but also in the criminal justice system. Jill Suttie in her article "Four Ways Teachers Can Reduce Implicit Bias" admits that there is bias within the educational system, and if left unchecked, the consequences could have a negative impact (pp. 1–3). Suttie offers methods to reduce prejudice and subconscious bias.

1) Cultivate awareness of their bias.
2) Work to increase empathy and empathic communications.
3) Practice mindfulness and loving-kindness.
4) Develop cross-group friendships in their own lives.

Safir and Suttie articles develop a foundation for further conversation and analysis. The complexity of the issues facing societal influence is discussed in Shelby Steele's book *White Guilt: How Blacks and Whites Together Destroyed the Promise of the Civil Rights Era.* Steele writes about his personal experiences throughout his life and how his mindset was influenced by societal actions (2006). In another book by Steele, *The Content of Our Character*, he questions or infers the premise of "white privilege" as a means for the underachievement of minorities to "white guilt" as a method to repay the Black community for previous indiscretions. "The self-preoccupied form of white guilt that is behind racial preferences always makes us lower so that we can be lifted up" (1990, 90). Steele refers to entitlements and affirmative action as a direct result of "white guilt" (p.112).

Thomas Sowell, in his book *Black Rednecks and White Liberals*, identifies major actions, policies, and trends that have hindered education for not only minorities but for all. He describes successful schools that were shut down or reorganized to meet the needs of the Department of Educational, which resulted in deficient academic rating (pp. 204–214). Jason L. Riley further endorses both Sowell and Shelby in his book *Please Stop Helping Us* by offering further insights as to societal influence on the academic performance of minorities, especially Black Americans. Societal influences, with some good intentions, have had negative results in the educational experience and the academic performance of not only minority students but all students regardless of race or ethnic background. The influence of bias, White privilege or guilt, the perceived need for affirmative action and entitlements became topics for discussion with the female inmates in the jail facility. The emphasis was on their K-12 educational experiences.

Public K-12 Experience

Public K-12 education is the key factor in determining positive or negative outcomes facing society. "The School to Prison Pipeline, Explained" further stipulates that 31 percent of suspended seventh grade students repeat a grade compared to 5 percent who are not suspended. Twenty-three percent of the suspended students end up in the Juvenile Court System (Nelson). According to the National Adult Literacy Survey (NALS) conducted in 2003 and revised in 2013 stipulates the 70 percent of all incarcerated adults cannot read at a fourth grade level, "meaning they lack the reading skills to navigate many everyday tasks or hold down anything but lower (paying) jobs." The Bureau of Justice Statistics (2014) reports that 68 percent of incarcerated individuals are high school dropouts. Inmates who have not completed high school have a higher rate of recidivism, according to C. W. Harlow in his article "Education and Correctional Populations: Special Report" (2003).

Anna Aizer and Joseph Doyle write in "Juvenile Incarceration, Human Capital, and Future Crime: Evidence from Randomly Assigned Judges" that "juvenile incarceration results in large decreases in the likelihood of high school completion and large increases in the likelihood of adult incarceration" (pp.759–803).

> Nearly three-quarters (74 percent) of fourth-graders who scored at the low end of the NAEP scale (below the 25th percentile) on the most recent test were from low-income families, while only 23 percent of children from low-income families scored at the high end (above the 75th percentile).

This report was written by Leila Fiester, senior consultant to the Campaign for Grade-Level Reading, who sponsored the Annie E. Casey Foundation and author of *Early Warning: Why Reading by the End of Third Grade Matters* (2013, 3). Donald Hernandez further explains in his book *Double Jeopardy* the importance of the *Early Warning* study, stipulating that "74% of 3rd graders who read poorly still struggle in ninth grade, and third grade reading scores can predict a student's likelihood to graduate high school." With this data and previously mentioned, the question should be what the role and the solutions to the problems is facing the public educational system, especially in the inner cities and among different races and nationalities. Hopefully, through this research, there will be some insight as to the influence of public education on criminal activity focusing on societal needs.

Lance Lochner and Enrico Moretti wrote in "The Effect of Education on Crime: Evidence from Prison Inmates, Arrests, and Self-Reports" that a one-year increase in educational grade level could reduce arrest rates by 11 percent (p.18).

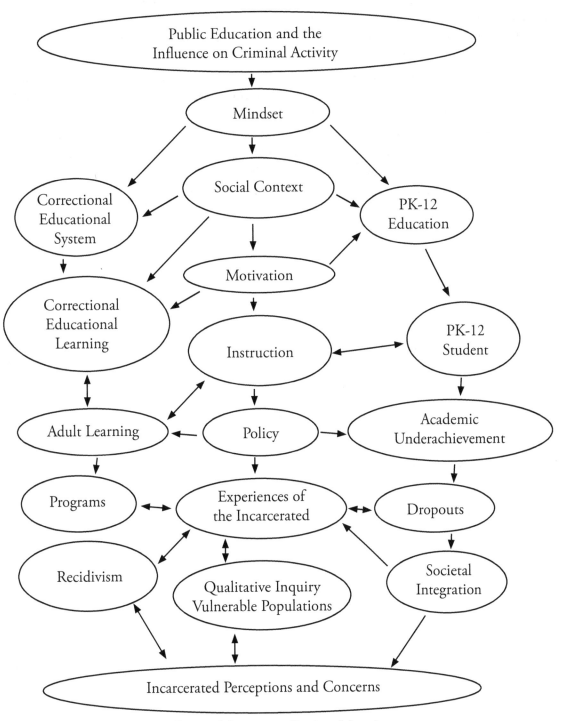

Figure 6. Literature Review Mapping

Summary

The literature review in chapters 1, 2, and 3 try to develop an understanding and appreciation for this research by developing a fundamental knowledge of the problems facing the incarcerated individual and just as important the problems facing society. The literature Review Map allows the individual to visualize the affect education has on the incarcerated individual, ranging from the importance of public education on the mindset of the incarcerated individual and the mindset of society in general. The societal perspective influences the mindset of the public school educational system as well as the correctional facilities. The literature review allows society to understand the difficulties and initiate a sense of urgency to collaboratively create a strategy or revised vision for the importance of a purpose and value-driven educational experience. There are still more questions that must be addressed by educators, administrators, and policymakers. What programs are the most effective curriculums for both public education and the correctional institutions? Can these curricular programs be linked to a singular database for common analysis?

CHAPTER 3

Methodology

Introduction

In this chapter, the emphasis is on operational design and how theoretical constructs are used to develop an outcome of understanding that has the potential to have an impact of initiating change. Chapter 3 will describe the contextual aspect of setting, participants, and the selection of participants. A pilot study is included that offers guidance as to the procedure and changes that must be made. The design includes narrative research, study questions, procedures, and rationale. Data collection and analysis includes first- and second-cycle coding and a procedural model. The role of the researcher involves trustworthiness, reflexivity, and ethical considerations. The methodology used addresses the validity and reliability of the research project.

Context

Chapter 2, the literature review, was based on theory to develop a foundation for research and clarity of understanding the *why* of the problems facing the incarcerated individual and society. The focus was on learning, motivation for incarcerated individuals, the public school, K-12 social context and policy. Prison-system education and the experiences of the incarcerated was addressed to understand current conditions and to further explore the mindset of the system and the individual student. A comparative analysis of international programs showed the importance of educational programing on changing the mindset of the individual. A qualitative inquiry was addressed to show the vulnerability of the incarcerated individual. The purpose of education in prison is to develop inmates' skills to achieve success in employment once released from prison.

According to Richard Goss in his article "Getting the Message Across," educational opportunities in prison should meet the needs of employers. "Most employers would like to employ ex-offenders but lack the confidence in the education they receive in prison" (Goss, 42–43). The question is *why*. The limitations of the prison educational system allow for testing to the text, so the individual can pass and get their high school equivalency diploma to get a job. Emphasis is on course material, not explaining why the course material is important. The purpose of learning is to change behavior and to answer the questions Who am I? Where am I going? How will I get there? John Hattie, in his book *Visible Learning for Teachers*, offers advice for instructors to establish beneficial interactions with students by clarifying "where am I going, how am I going to get there, and where to next" in setting goals and expectations (pp. 130–132).

Setting

The setting for this research is at high-security jail and prison facilities. All individuals—including prison administrators, guards, staff/personnel, instructors, chaplains, contractors, and volunteers—must go through the central checkpoint. At the entrance, everyone must go through a metal detector and be frisked. Once approved for entrance, all doors and gates are opened by a security guard monitoring all locations of the facility. Inside the facility, hallways are sectioned off with gates to prevent too many people from gathering at one time in one area. Inmates walk in lines and are not permitted to talk to anyone, unless they are addressed to by a person of authority. There are usually four units or pods in one building that houses approximately eighty individuals. The inmates live in a stark nonpersonalized cell with a metal bed, sink, and toilet. They can have a small locker for personal belongings. The classroom is considered by some to be a safe zone where they can escape the realities of prison. In the classroom, the inmates have access to computers that have limited capabilities and are controlled by the facility officials. The classroom usually has a capacity of fifteen to twenty students.

Participants

The participants are from two groups. The females are in the county jail facility and the males are incarcerated in the maximum-security state prison. All individuals have opted to participate in the GED or HiSET educational programs. A small number of individuals have been court-ordered to take the classes in hopes of rehabilitating the individual's mindset from criminality to being productive members of society. The female participants' age ranged from eighteen to thirty-five, with an average age of twenty-nine. They have not completed their high school degree but were enrolled in the purpose- and values-driven educational preparatory class. Their crimes ranged from armed assault, child neglect, drug usage and distribution, and robbery. The male participants volunteered for the questionnaire segment so they can be included in the findings of this study. The men have been released from the DOC prison facilities and are on parole. The average age is thirty-seven, and the crimes committed range from armed assault, robbery, drug distribution, and attempted murder.

Selection of Participants

The selection of participants is critical to the success of the research project. Female students were selected from the County Sheriff's Office and were presently enrolled in the High School Equivalency Test (HiSET) diploma program. Age is relevant since the students have recently attended public schools, but just as important is the factor that their children are now enrolled in school. The participants were presently enrolled in my educational classes, and this is important because I have been able to develop a rapport with the students, and they felt confident in discussing the experiences. This narrative research is a highly personal disclosure and requires an intimate approach that requires a high degree of sensitivity on the part of the researcher.

Male parolees were previously enrolled in the researchers Parenting from Prison program at the Department of Corrections (DOC) and were selected to answer the research questions in a written-essay format. The purpose of the male questionnaire was to see if there was a correlation between the experiences of female and male inmates. This was a voluntary participation program for both men and women. All participants were informed of their rights, and permission had already been granted from the county and the state correctional authorities.

J. W. Creswell, in his book *Educational Research: Planning, Conducting, and Evaluating Quantitative and Qualitative Research*, 4th edition (2012), defined a culture-sharing group as "two or more individuals who shared behaviors, beliefs, and language" (p. 469). The cultural makeup of this study were Caucasian, African American, and Hispanic students who attended public schools but maybe do not share the same behaviors, beliefs, and language. The commonality was that they attended public school but did not graduate. An additional participant and observer includes a teacher, Ms. Tiffany Manning, who has been working at the facility and has developed a strong rapport with the inmates. Her empathy for her students and her experience in the public school of frustrations and poor academics was an example for the students that if a person wants to succeed, they can. Ms. Manning was an asset for this research.

In this section, a description of the participants and how they are selected to be part of this research is provided. At the County Sheriff's Office facility for women, the selected inmates were presently enrolled in the HiSET diploma program. An initial questionnaire was given to the individuals to answer the questions (see Appendix 6) in essay format. They were given a week to answer the questions with an emphasis on responding with their initial reaction and not the answer they think the researcher wants to read. Once the essays had been collected, a focus-group session was conducted to offer clarification of the experiences and to try to develop a potential solution.

The focus-group participants included all the students who answered the questionnaire. Two or three individuals were selected for further interviews and a more in-depth explanation for their answers and experiences. Their answers reflect the responses of the other participants but offer an interesting story of their personal experiences. The paroled male participants were given the same questionnaire as the women and given the same instructions to complete the essays. The answers were compared to the women's to see if there is a correlation and similarity of their experiences. This inquiry was voluntary, and all the participants gave verbal approval, as directed by the IRB. The names were collected and will be secured with the appropriate authorities. For security and confidentiality purposes, the names will not be included in this research report, unless permission is granted by the participants.

Pilot Study

A pilot study was initiated to determine the feasibility of the research question and establish guidelines for further research. The study was beneficial in that it provided an insight to the thought process of inmates and allowed for the revision of questions and procedures for the main research question. The focus-groups sessions were held on February 20 and 27, 2017, to determine if there was any correlation between the public school experience and criminal activity. Four male students and one female instructor participated in the first session. In this session, general noneducational questions were asked to help prepare the members to be open and candid about their answers.

The first series of questions asked were as follows:

1) What is creativity?
2) Are you born with creativity?
3) Can you lose the ability to be creative?
4) Can one develop creativity later in life?

During the second session, another male student joined the group, and questions about educational experiences were discussed.

1) What was your educational experience in public schools?
2) What was your experience like with teachers?
3) What was your educational experience like with other classmates?

(See appendix A for a complete list of questions.)

These questions are based on a reflective interview approach as defined by Michael Patton in *Qualitative Research and Evaluation Methods* (p. 462). In this focus-group study, the interviews were conducted with the assistance of Tiffany Manning, an instructor with the County Sheriff's Office, and five inmate students seeking their HiSET diploma. The participants were informed that this was an informal interview of their perception of their educational experiences in the public school system and the possible influence it had on criminal activity. Permission to conduct the interview was sought and the confirmation that it was completely voluntary on their part.

The first focus-group session was held at the county training facility on February 20, 1017, and lasted twenty-six minutes and thirty-seven seconds. In this study, the focus was on the students and an instructor to establish their perceptions as to the effectiveness of the HiSET program and assessments to gather in-depth analysis to determine a course for action and a solution for the problems facing not only the students but also correctional institutions, public education, and society in general. This study utilized analysis of interpretation to establish the effectiveness of the program and offer a portrait of the current conditions and develop a narrative to initiate change. The focus-group process offered a narrative storytelling approach to further understand the prison culture and students' and instructors' feelings toward education. Some of the answers to the questions and in the focus-group discussion helped clarify the need for further research and supported the research question for this project.

Focus-Group Sample of Responses from the Pilot Study

P-1. "I attended eight different schools and never fit in anyplace."
P-2. "I really liked my second-grade teacher. She encouraged me"
P-3. "Most of my teachers were angry. Maybe it was me."
P-4. "The other students made fun of me because of my clothes."
P-5. "I talked back and got into trouble. I got kicked out, and I spent more time on the streets than in school."
P-6. "I was bored."
P-7. "I did not want to say I did not understand the assignment."

More importantly, this study develops a foundation for an action-, research-based study to initiate change from penance to rehabilitation by analyzing the outcomes. The utilization of interviews, assessments, and participant observations offers themes and theories to initiate a course of action. As the study was being conducted, the realization became apparent that there is potential to develop a greater understanding of the problems facing not only the correctional department but also society in general.

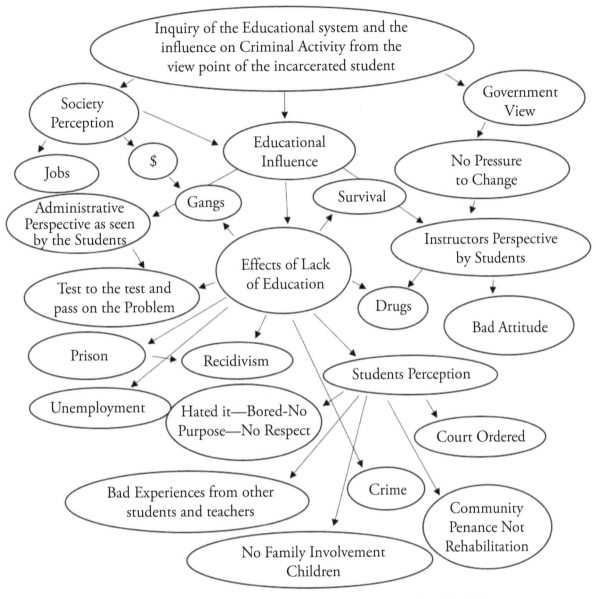

Figure 7. Pilot Mapping: Inquiry of Inmates Perception of Public Education
and the Influence It Had on Their Criminal Activities

The pilot study indicated that there are several problems facing the incarcerated individual, and more research must be utilized to develop a social constructivist approach to improve the learning environment.

Research Design

This study was a designed-based research as defined by Joseph Maxwell in *Qualitative Research Design: An Interactive Approach* (2nd edition) with the emphasis on students' previous interactions with instructors and administration in the public-school system (p.7). The core to this research was a narrative inquiry to explore the behaviors, values, attitudes, and experiences of incarcerated individuals in their relation to their educational experiences in the public school system. According to Maxwell (2005), qualitative analysis should begin with a foundation that already supports the study. To establish this foundation, two qualitative studies were conducted and applied to develop a foundation of support for this research. The two studies were conducted to create awareness of the problems or concerns in the educational programing at the Sheriff's Office facilities. In the fall of 2016, a request was made to incorporate the level of education completed by all individuals arrested in county into the county database. This request was granted and went into effect on January 1, 2017.

This study determined if there was a correlation between the level of education completed, age, and crimes committed. The second study requested was to determine to the level of comprehension for students enrolling in the HiSET program. In this assessment, students are required to take the Test of Adult Basic Intelligence (TABE 9/10 D). This indicated the grade equivalency and also helped prepare lesson plans per one's comprehension of the courses. The grade-level equivalency assessment went into effect in the fall of 2016. The data provided by the Sheriff's Office will be a valuable resource for further structural development of educational programing. With this foundation or knowledge of grade school equivalency, more research can be initiated to further understand where the students are academically, and qualitative analysis can be utilized to further understand the mindset of the students, as well as the course structure. The two added data resources are essential to the design of this project to build a foundation of knowledge and understanding. To further clarify this research focus and design, a logical model of potential outcomes for the research project has been included.

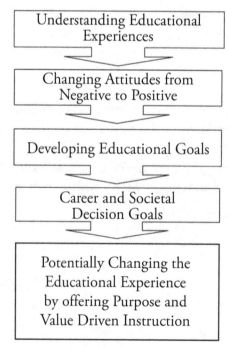

Figure 8. Logical Model for Potential Outcomes

Narrative Research

The inquiry into this narrative research was to study how different individuals experienced their education in public schools. This study allowed the students who are incarcerated to tell their stories of their educational experiences. The design was focused on the experiences of the student-inmates and their chronological context using the technique of retelling their experiences to construct a collaborative narrative account. The goal of this narrative research design was to collaboratively explore past experiences to understand the impact on the present situation and potentially change the future.

The research contained three stages consisting of questionnaire, interviews, and a focus-group session that offered an opportunity for the inmates to reflect, compare experiences, and possibly offer solutions. The first stage of this intensive study was to discuss with female students in the researcher's *practical, purposeful,* and *value-driven* GED program at the county jail facility the importance of education. The group met weekly and had not been told of this research until a rapport had been developed in the fourth week. The male parolees from a DOC prison facility who had participated in a Parenting from Prison program were invited to participate, and a relation had already been established. Questionnaires pertaining to experiences in the public education were given to all participants who had volunteered for this study (see appendix B).

A voluntary focus group of fourteen participants was conducted after the initial questionnaire process. Members of the focus group were selected for the interview process, and the narrative interviews and a focus-group inquiry were used to develop a portrait of the effectiveness of public school educational experiences ranging from course material, teacher experience, student interactions, and the organizational structure of the school. The results of the interviews, focus group, and questionnaire were compared to determine if there is a pattern and theme to the effectiveness of the educational process and experience. The focus group consisted of all races with an emphasis on Caucasian, Hispanic, and African American students.

The researcher conducted the focus group-sessions due the confidence level that had been gained from knowing the inmates in a classroom setting. Access to the education grade equivalency results, which are recorded into a database, was made available. Mixed methodology of the use of quantitative statistics already supplied by the Sheriff's Office and the Department of Corrections was utilized to offer further clarification of the educational background of the participants. Narrative approach was utilized to determine a theory and/or theme of the correlation between the influence of educational experiences in the public school system and criminal activities. The following graphic conceptual design was not the focus of this study but a benefit as to the reasoning and logic for meaningful and purpose-driven educational reform. Figures 8 and 9 show the conceptual design of the benefits of this research study.

Conceptual Design and Purpose

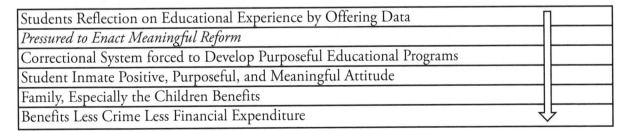

Figure 9. Conceptualization of Benefits of Purposeful Educational Reform

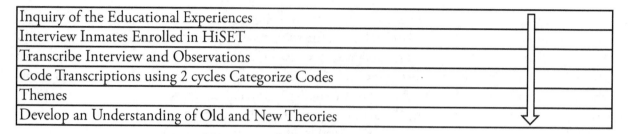

Inquiry of the Educational Experiences	
Interview Inmates Enrolled in HiSET	
Transcribe Interview and Observations	
Code Transcriptions using 2 cycles Categorize Codes	
Themes	
Develop an Understanding of Old and New Theories	

Figure 10. Conception of Qualitative Process

Research Question

The research was based on the perceptions of inmates on their educational experiences in the public school educational system and the influence it had on their criminal activity. The answers to these questions led to other questions that also had a contributing influence on criminal behavior. Factors such as family, community, peer pressure, and economics also became contributing agents that led to incarceration. The focus was on the influence of public school education, but the narrative inquiry led to further clarification for criminal behavior and offered solutions to correct the present situation. To further clarify the importance of the research question, potential outcomes directly developed an understanding of educational experiences that led to changing attitudes of incarcerated individuals. The research question developed higher aspirations by establishing goals that lead to career decisions and potentially offering insight to the importance of practical, purposeful, and value-driven instruction.

Overview of Present Conditions in Relation to the Research Question

The mission statement for the County Sheriff's Office states:

> As a law enforcement agency committed to public safety, we strive to be a leader in the field of corrections, service of civil process, and innovative community-based programs, emphasizing Accountability, Diversity, Integrity, Professionalism.

Within the organizational structure of the Sheriff's Office, an educational section has been established to assist inmates receive a high school equivalency diploma while they are incarcerated and after they have been released from jail. As previously stated, the main difficulty is that there is no financial assistance from the county or state to develop an effective educational program. There is no major emphasis by society, governmental officials, or the Department of Corrections on the benefits of educational programs for the incarcerated. A secondary purpose or vision of this study was to redefine the importance of education as a device to deter the recidivism rate for individuals who have been incarcerated by the county. Once inmates can motivate themselves to excel in education and prove their worth to society, then there would be motivation by society to develop practical, purposeful, and value-driven rehabilitation programs. The starting place to initiate change is understanding the mindset of the inmate.

Procedures of Understanding Basic Principles

As a person who has taught in the prison system, I have heard many stories as to the reasons why one was incarcerated and the problems that led to that incarceration. These stories have instilled a curiosity for more research to establish a theme in the experiences of inmates and to attempt to establish a common thread that could lead to a solution. The procedural methodology was incorporated with my personal observations into the study based on conversations that I have had with the incarcerated student. Bias that reform is needed in the educational programing of the correctional system has already been established, but for this study, an open mind was used to the questionnaire, focus group, and interview questions and outcomes.

Focus-group sessions were conducted to determine the mindset of the individual from previous educational experiences and allow students to share their personal stories. The main reason for the focus group was to validate the narrative interviews and that there was a consensus of opinions. This action research captured some of the truth and reality of the situation and offers potential solutions to the situation, but there are limits based on the design. The principles of triangulation to ensure accuracy were used to verify respondent validation and adequate engagement on data collection (Patton, 386). Triangulation was important to receive validation from another source. In this study, the participant's response was compared to other participants,' with personal observations as the third form of triangulation.

According to Patton, direct observation can add valuable knowledge as to what happened and, more importantly, *why* it happened (p. 585). The researcher cannot be biased or have preconceived notions that will have a bearing on the results. The respondent validation was useful to further engage in meaningful dialogue. Adequate engagement of data allowed for proper interpretation. The students were given an opportunity to confirm or deny actual findings and confirm that the statement was accurate. The third aspect was the adequate engagement with the participants. The researcher must develop a rapport with the students and gain their confidence. We know little about why students chose a life of crime and if there is any correlation between educational experiences and criminal activity. The contextual design of this research supported or diminished the inmate-student's perception of their educational experience as a catalyst for criminal activity. Merriam (2009) explains that qualitative researchers

> are interested in how people interpret their experiences, how they construct their worlds, what meaning they attribute to their experiences. The overall purposes of qualitative research are to achieve an understanding of how people make sense out of their lives, delineate the process (rather than the outcome or product) of meaning-making, and describe how people interpret what they experience. (p. 14)

This qualitative narrative approach added clarity and a different perspective to information that is underrepresented in literature.

Process Model—Initial Steps in the Process

Identify the purpose of the research project and explain to the participants

⇩

Develop initial research questions

⇩

Obtain necessary permission and have participants understand that this research is voluntary and will follow ethical guidelines

⇩

Establish a relationship of trust and confidentiality with participants that is mutually constructed and characterized by an equality of voice

⇩

Submit research questions to the participants

⇩

Develop a focus group of all the participants to offer clarification and support by collaborating with the participants to validate the accuracy of their story

⇩

Identify 2 or 3 individuals who can elaborate and become storytellers of their experiences for the narrative interviews

Figure 11. Process Model

Rationale

"Eyes cannot see what the mind is not open to. It's like out of mind, out of sight. Similarly, the mind cannot see what the eye is not open to. Which means out of sight, out of mind. The statement 'Eyes are blind to what the mind cannot see' applies to our negligence" (Stevie Wonder).

The rationale for using the coding and categorization cycles is that the researcher can record and transcribe words, thoughts, phrases, and sentences from interviews and funnel these expressions from chaos into a meaningful process of initiating possible solutions to the research question. Creswell's organizational structure of defining the setting or environment, identifying characters or individuals who have a narrative story, explaining the actions or behavior, describing the problems, and offering resolution could initiate a solution to the research question (Creswell, 511).

Table 3. Problem Narrative Structure
Organizing the Story Elements into the Problem-Solution Narrative Structure

Settings	Characters	Actions	Problems	Resolutions
Context, environment, conditions, place, time, locale, year, and era	Individuals in the story described as archetypes, personalities, their behaviors, style, and patterns	Movements of individuals through the story illustrating the character's thinking or behaviors	Questions to be answered or phenomena to be described or explained	Answers to questions and explanations about what caused the character to change

Data Collection

Once the questionnaire essay answers had been collected, the responses were compared to establish a common theme among the participants (appendix B). The coding and categorization of the answers to the questionnaire was similar to the focus group and interview process, but not as intensive. The essay answers were recorded and analyzed to find commonality of themes. The value of the questionnaire was to find similarities of experiences regarding behavior, values, expectations, educational experiences, group dynamics, family influence, and peer pressure. Once again, the purpose of the questionnaire was to select candidates for the focus group and interview process who have stories to tell.

Focus-Group Design

The focus group was conducted with all willing participants who were participants in the HiSET class and inmates who initially answered the research questionnaire. The main purpose was to develop a discussion about their educational experiences and the relation it had on their criminal activity. Norms and expectations were established to offer guidelines for discussion, as described by Richard Dufour, Rebecca Dufour, and Robert Eaker in their book *Revisiting Professional Learning Communities at Work* (2008, 284). This discussion was an organized forum allowing participants to offer feedback without interruption but also offering an opportunity for others to respond. Another purpose was to allow the participants to tell their story using emotion as a device to address the concerns of both the mind and heart.

The guidelines for this focus group were influenced by Richard A. Krueger in his book *Using Stories in Evaluation* (2010, 404–405). Krueger's argues that storytelling can illustrate key points and themes that offer clarification and support. Another purpose, and was the most important, was that the individuals are taking ownership in the discussion and that they are part of program that could influence a dynamic change in educational instruction. The focus group was not the main element of this research. It was a device to compare a group discussion with the narrative responses.

Interview Process

The interview process was the focal point of this research. The two candidates were selected from their answers from the questionnaire, the focus-group session, and their participation in classroom activities. An emphasis on their storytelling ability and their experiences determined selection to the interview process. The questions for the interview were based on the guidelines to stimulate responses to develop further questions for clarification. Patton suggested six types of questions (2015):

1. Experience and behavior
2. Opinion and values
3. Feelings
4. Knowledge
5. Sensory
6. Background

Once the candidates had been selected and interviewed, a period was offered to discuss their answers and to offer further clarification. Everyone was interviewed separately and given the time needed to complete the process by being allowed to tell their story using real-life experiences and analogies to develop a clear and concise portrait of their situation. The interview process was recorded and transcribed to offer ethical authenticity to the process (see appendix B for list of questions).

Data Analysis

After recording and transcribing the interview, the first cycle for analyzation were the *in vivo*, *process*, and *value coding*. Emotional coding or the ability to recall experiences, values to be able to reflect on attitudes, and the final analysis will be versus coding to determine the thought process inmates toward teachers and the administration. The anticipated categories from the pilot study that were explored are student's experiences and reflections of their educational experiences that might have influenced their criminal activity, including demographics, interactions with other criminals, response to teachers and administration, response to other students, and family background.

Due to active teaching in the prison classroom and observing the participants, a semantic structure of analysis was incorporated to see if there are patterns of shared meaning, as described by J. P. Spradley in his book *Participant Observation* (1980, 85–91). Even though the semantic structure is for ethnographic study, it became a valuable tool for further analyzation of this narrative project. The semantic structure allowed the observer to develop an understanding of different the backgrounds and cultures of the participants, the relation between the data, and the emergence of themes for coding. The three stages of analysis are as follows:

1) Domain analysis, where one can identify categories of cultural meaning
2) Taxonomic analysis by developing relationships between the data
3) Componential analysis, which can determine patterns of emerging themes

By utilizing these three stages of analysis, the researcher began to develop an understanding of the mindset of the incarcerated individual and offer a course of action. According to Spradley, there are two levels of cultural knowledge that must be utilized by the researcher to fully understand the mindset and motives of the participants. Explicit and tacit levels could cause different interpretations of the same topic. The explicit is the knowledge that is stated precisely, leaving no room for confusion or misunderstanding, whereas tacit knowledge is more implied and due to silence or nonverbal gestures that could have a different interpretation of meaning (Spradley 1980, 7–8).

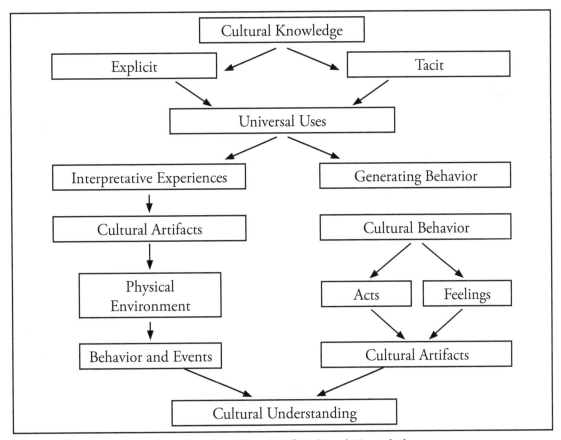

Figure 12. Two Levels of Cultural Knowledge

The greater the cultural knowledge by the researcher allows for more accurate interpretations in the coding process. The first phase was to gather raw information or data from the interview participants and the observer. Secondly, begin to take key words or phrases and turn them into codes, which determined the third step of creating categories. The fourth step was to construct concepts that have direct meaning and impact.

First-Cycle Analysis

The methodological step in the first cycle was to code the transcripts and observer's memos into meaningful comments that were used to develop categories, themes, and theories. The first cycle of coding was established by using in vivo or actual language of the transcript and memos to develop a framework for interpret meanings. The second code was the process or action analysis to determine what was occurring in the educational process and/or other factors. The third phase in the first cycle is the initial code by breaking down the words into discrete units for analysis (*see* figure 12).

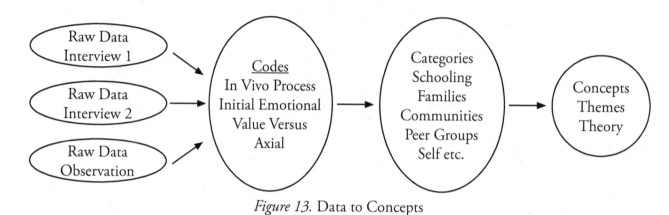

Figure 13. Data to Concepts

Second-Cycle Analysis

The second cycle of coding offered clarification and meaning to the true story or message of the interview by using emotional, value, and versus, and coding. Due to the interview and focus-group responses, an axial code was added to show the interaction between various individuals or groups. The next step was to determine categories for the codes and begin to create and interpret actual meanings. Additional categories that were incorporated also related back to the initial research question. The influence of the family, self, peers, and community allowed for further scrutiny in developing an actual answer to the original research question. This allowed for the formation of an organizational structure for developing concepts and themes. As these codes, categories, and themes start to emerge, the cycle process began to establish meaning. With these themes, the educational influences were exposed, but also other influences as to what caused criminal behavior emerged. Influences such as family, community, peers, and self-efficacy allowed for the formation of new theories to be developed that influenced criminal behavior. These themes helped understand the mindset of the individual students. An important concept developed by allowing the participants to offer solutions to improve the educational system in public schools and at the correctional training facility, but also solutions for the family, community, peers, and self. The importance of this methodology approach was that it developed clarity of the project and a foundation for further research (*see* figure 14).

Model of Data Analysis

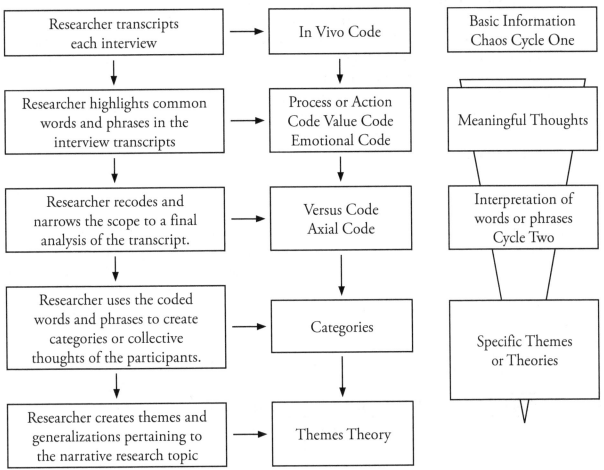

Figure 14. Data Analysis Process. Adapted and modified from A. Strauss and J. Corbin's "Eight Steps of Data Analysis Procedure."

Researcher's Role

The researcher relates both the description and the themes back to a larger portrait of what was learned, which often reflects some combination of the researcher making a personal assessment, returning to the literature on the cultural theme and raising further questions based on the data. It might also include addressing problems (Creswell, 473). To achieve this goal, a researcher must be able to adapt and meet the needs of the participants. A researcher must be able to establish norms and expectations for not only the group but for the individual. The interviews must be informative and created out of curiosity from the researcher to be able to explore deeper into the mindset and answers of the participants.

Working with incarcerated individuals is a challenge. They are interested in changing their actions from a negative to a positive, but they are not sure, or they lack the confidence as to how. Every time they enter a classroom, their attitude could be entirely different that the time before. That is due to the experiences in the unit or their cells. The researcher must be able to recognize the difference and be prepared to alter the questions or negate them altogether and just have a conversation that leads to the questions. The mental and physical conditions of the participant might negate the viability and accuracy of an interview. The flexibility for the researcher is to recognize the present condition and postpone the interview for another time. The importance of this recognition must be supported by Maslow's Hierarchy of Needs so the participant an achieve self-actualization. The use of the Rogerian principles of finding common ground and a sense of purpose is important for the participant to achieve self-worth (Rogers 1956). The flexibility of the researcher is to recognize the personality trait in each individual and be able to adapt to their needs. To achieve this goal, a researcher must have flexibility in connection with the participants. Action research, as described by Richard Sagor in his book *Guiding School Improvement*, is defined as "a disciplined process of inquiry conducted by and for those taking action. The primary reason for engaging in action research is to assist the 'actor' in improving and /or refining his or her actions."

Trustworthiness

The trustworthiness of this research study is important to academic world in the public school system, correctional institutions educational programs, and to society in general so that further research and discussion can be conducted on this topic. The purpose of trustworthiness in a qualitative inquiry is to support the inquiry's findings and to guarantee the study has validity and is reliable for other research projects (Lincoln and Guba 1985). Based on Lincoln and Guba's research, trustworthiness involves establishing four main criteria:

Table 4. Criteria Trustworthiness—Four Main Criteria

Credibility	Transferability	Dependability	Conformability
Confidence in the "truth" of the findings	The ability to show the findings have applicability in other contexts	The research shows the findings are consistent and could be replicated	The degree of neutrality or the extent to which the findings of a study are shaped by the respondents and not biased by the researcher's motivation or interest
The viability of the research must be based on accuracy of recording data, not based on bias or misleading information. To ensure accuracy, the researcher must be accountable for recording data by evaluating the four main criteria for each entry.			

There is another aspect of trustworthiness and that is the relation of researcher to the participants. Trust must be developed to achieve reliable and valid results. The participants must feel that they are serving a purpose and that their responses have meaning. Their responses must be sincere and accurate. By developing this interactive trust between the researcher and the participants, the trustworthiness of the study can be challenged, but the challenges can be responded to in an intellectual manner by supplying credibility, consistency, and transferability (Merriam, p.242).

Reflexivity

"The researcher being aware of and openly discussing his or her role in the study in a way that honors and respects the site and participants" (Creswell, 474). The purpose of this narrative research is relatively simple: develop an understanding of the mindset of the incarcerated individual toward public education and potentially find a solution to the problem of educational experiences and the influence on criminal activity. The researcher should not try to influence the outcomes of the interviews with questions that are leading or show bias toward the research question. One must to remain neutral, but this is difficult in that the researcher has become part of the study with "a powerful and inescapable influence" (Maxwell, 109). The researcher must be cognizant of how one is influencing the outcomes of the responses and try to minimize the effect and how the influence affects the validity of the research question. Even though there is a perceived bias as to the present structure for educational programs in public schools, prisons, and jail facilities, this research must be conducted from an open-minded position of no preconceived notions. The research will also be exploring the constructivist theory of participants using the knowledge they already know and applying that knowledge to further construct new forms of teaching and learning. This approach can be useful not only for instructors but also for students. The comparing and contrasting teaching and learning experiences can be used to initiate a change in the mindset of the individual.

Ethical Considerations

This narrative inquiry approach inevitably leads to questions about the validity of the narratives told by participants, including the question of whether or not they represent memory reconstruction versus "facts" (Clandinin and Connolly 2001). The narrative inquiry of this project demands ethical standards for all aspects of the study. Institutional Review Board (IRB), County Sheriff's Office, and the Department of Corrections all have ethical standards that must be followed. These standards will offer reliability, credibility, and validity to the research. Patton offers twelve basic principles that offers a guideline or checklist for ethical issues (2014, 496):

1. Explaining purpose or expected value
2. Reciprocity
3. Promises
4. Risk assessment
5. Confidentiality
6. Informed consent
7. Data access
8. Interviewer mental health
9. Ethical advice
10. Data collection
11. Intersection of ethical and methodological choices
12. Ethic versus legal

Figure 15. Twelve Ethical Issues Checklist

Each one of these issues must be addressed to all active participants. By clarifying the ethical standards for this research project, we have anticipated dilemmas and can deal with ethical dimensions of this narrative inquiry.

Summary

The inquiry into this narrative research was to develop an understanding of the mindset of the incarcerated individual towards public education and potentially find a solution to the problem of educational experiences and the influence on criminal activity. In this chapter, a description of the methodology that guided this research project was based on the findings and procedures conducted in the pilot study and adapted to clarify the primary research question and, more importantly, the additional subquestions that developed. Interpreting and representing another person's thoughts and experiences was not an easy task, but it is rewarding. By following the principles and guidelines in this chapter, we enabled the participants to develop a sense of self-worth and that, by participating in this project, their responses could have a positive impact on the educational system in our society.

CHAPTER 4

Research Findings

The primary research question was an inquiry into inmates' perceptions of public school education and the influence it had on their criminal activity. The research was divided into five separated sections, ranging from the equity audit, questionnaire, focus group, two interviews, and classroom discussions. The purpose was to develop a funnel of information leading to possible solutions provided by the inmates and to analytically change the mindset of the individual from self-centered to a greater cause of family, peers, community, and the importance of education. The equity audit provided a foundation of knowledge and a database that proved to helpful in developing an understanding of the situation and helped develop solutions to the problems facing the incarcerated individuals and their children.

Equity Audits

Most of the subquestions were anticipated due to the equity audit that was conducted prior to the questionnaire, focus-group session, and interviews. The subquestion that came after the questionnaire and focus-group session was the importance of one's perception of self. The purpose was to develop an understanding of the mindset of the individuals toward educational experiences, and equity audits were conducted to establish a foundation for the conditions that could have contributed to the reasons for their behavior (see appendix F for equity audit process). The Equity-Oriented Change Agent (EOCA) became a guiding attribute to initiate conversations and a course of action to develop a cooperative approach to the understanding of the problems and to develop positive outcomes for the incarcerated individual and the educational system (Skrla, 70–79).

Research for this project was initiated in 2015, and new databases were incorporated by the DCSO to assist in the pilot study for this research. The first equity audit was conducted in March of 2017 of Davidson County, Tennessee, and statistics were gathered to develop a picture of the demographics and to determine if any factor contributed to the educational competency could have an impact on the problems in the community. Some of the important findings were that of similar cities, such as St. Louis, Missouri, and Milwaukee, Wisconsin. As of July 2016, the population of Davison County was 684,410 with a median age of thirty-three years. Males made up 48.4 percent of the population while females were at 51.6 percent. The racial breakdown is 57.4 percent White, 27.54 percent Black, 9.8 percent Hispanic, 3 percent Asian, and 1.9 percent other races. The median income is $51,000 while 17.6 percent of the workforce earns less than $26,000 per year.

The interesting statistic supplied by the DCSO was that 76 percent of the incarcerated inmates in the DCSO facilities do not have a high school degrees and are from low-income communities.

To further analyze the Davidson County and the demographics of the population, data was gathered to as to the racial makeup of the community, school districts, and location of criminal activity. The population is segregated into racial communities, like Milwaukee and St. Louis. In Davidson County, the southeast corridor is primarily Hispanic, with the northern, eastern, western, and southern precincts Black. The White population is congregated around Nashville and is segregated with the other races. Further analysis was made of the school districts and the degree of academic competency in relation to criminal activity.

There are thirty-five districts in Davidson County with a school enrollment of 84,069 students. The academic rating by the state gives Davidson County a C+ with teachers receiving a B- and the administration a B+. The reading proficiency is 41 percent, and math-proficiency rating was 48 percent. An audit of low-performing schools based on location was similar to the racial makeup of the communities with the Black and Hispanic community districts scoring the lowest-performing ratings.

To further funnel down the data into meaningful and logical perspectives, an analysis of criminal activity by zip code compared the segregated areas and the low-performing school districts as the locations for the greatest amount of crime. The question prevails if there is a relationship between incarceration and education. The statistics previously reported that 76 percent of the inmates in the Davidson County facilities do not have a high school degree is very prevalent in the correlation between education and incarceration. This preliminary audit of the community was used just to be able to offer an insight as to the present conditions of the educational environment of the DCSO and funnel down data to provide a picture of the aptitude and attitude of the inmates, administration, and instructors. The inmate population at the Davidson County facilities is 3,551, which 99 percent are classified as adults: 87.7 percent are males, and 12.3 percent are female. White inmates make 44.3 percent and blacks at 37.7 percent. Hispanics make up 15.8 percent of the incarcerated population. Fifty-three percent of people in prison earned less than $10,000 per year before incarceration ("The Economic Costs of Childhood Poverty in the United States," *The Journal of Children and Poverty*).

The first major change to the DCSO database was the inclusion of information as to the grade level completed by incarcerated individuals at time of booking. To further verify the accuracy of the information gathered, an audit was conducted of inmates based on their past educational experience. In the pilot study, the DCSO asked inmates to voluntarily declare their grade completed at time of arrest. Of the 135 respondents, 77 percent said they did not complete high school; 43 percent of the individuals who did not complete high school got to the twelfth grade but did not graduate. Twenty-three percent indicated they attended some college (see appendix F).

In March, April, and May of 2017, permission was granted to test twenty-two women inmates from one class at the beginning of the session. Seven White, nine African American, and six Hispanic individuals were asked what the highest grade was they attended in school, where they lived, and what school they attended. Two or 9.10 percent were from out of state but committed the crimes in the Broadway area of Nashville. Three or 13.6 percent grew up in affluent areas surrounding Nashville but committed the crimes in the South Precinct crime-labeled area of Nashville. Seventeen or 77.3 percent lived in the school district with low ratings and committed the crimes in those areas. The White students indicated that they attended school until the 7.6 grade, the Blacks 11.2 grade, and the Hispanics 6.2 grade. Grade level is reported at time of arrest. Most of the arrests are of individuals in the twenty to twenty-nine age bracket and indicate that they attended school until the twelfth grade but did not receive a diploma (the results and process are reported in appendix F).

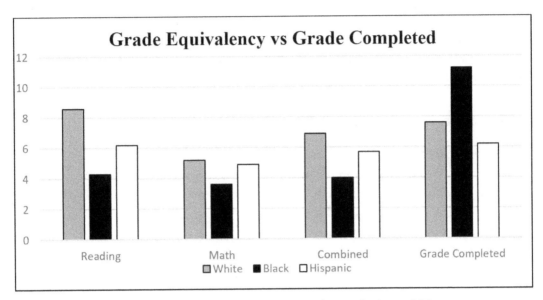

Figure 16. Achievement Gap between White, Black, and Hispanic Races: Grade Equivalency vs. Grade Completed

The risk ratio is shown in table 6 and indicates a wide separation between the academic achievement of the different races with a risk ratio in reading of 1.65 and in math 1.19 between White and Black students. The ratio between White and Hispanic was not as dramatic, but still indicated a concern. The risk ratio between White and Hispanic was in reading 1.38 and in math 0.89. The combined risk ratio between White and Black students was 1.72; between White and Hispanic was 1.21. The ratio between Hispanic and Blacks was 1.40, with the Hispanics outscoring the Black students in both categories. The importance of this data is that it indicated the probability of potential outcomes and offers areas of concern that can be addressed to decrease the risk ratio to a more equitable proportion of educational needs.

Table 5. *Risk Ratio*
Risk Ratio (.25 Difference is an area of concern)

Reading	White / Black	(1.65)		
	White / Hispanic	(1.38)		
Math	White / Black	(1.19)		
	White / Hispanic	(0.89)		
Combined	White / Black	(1.72)		
	White / Hispanic	(1.21)		
Scores				
White	Reading	8.6	Math	5.2
Black	Reading	4.3	Math	3.6
Hispanic	Reading	6.2	Math	4.9

The academic proficiency data gathered from the DCSO is similar to the Florida Department of Corrections 2011 annual report which indicated that 71.7 percent of incarcerated individuals test at a sixth grade or below GED preparation level (p. 34). The DCSO data indicates that individuals tested have an accumulative grade level literacy of 6.4. To further offer clarification of this phenomenon, questionnaires and interviews were conducted to determine and understand the why literacy is only 6.4 grade level for incarcerated individuals and to establish if there is a relation between education and criminal activity.

Questionnaire and Interview Research Process

The interview research process was conducted in four stages. The first stage was a structured questionnaire to establish a foundation for further study. The second stage was the focus-group discussion to clarify the findings of the questionnaire. In the third stage, individuals were selected for a more comprehensive and unstructured interview process. Due to the nature of the responses, an addition segment was included to provide classroom discussion and feedback to the responses made in the previous segments of research.

Questionnaire

The structured questions and answers, including essay answers, were recorded and analyzed to find commonality of themes. The value of the questionnaire was to find similarities of experiences regarding behavior, values, expectations, educational experiences, group dynamics, family influence, and peer pressure. Once again, the purpose of the questionnaire was to select candidates for the interview process who have stories to tell. There were twenty-six participants from the DCSO women's facility, of which eleven were Caucasians, eight African Americans, six Hispanic, and one Asian, with a combined average age of thirty-three. Twenty-four lived within the city limits of Nashville, one suburban and one rural. There were seven males who belong to a mentorship program and have just been recently released from Department of Correction facilities. There were three Caucasians, two blacks, and two Hispanics. Six of the participants committed crimes in Davidson County, Tennessee, and one from the Texas prison system. The questionnaire results were recorded using actual written responses and developing process, axial, emotion, values, and versus codes. The primary category of public school experiences was based on the research question as an inquiry to the inmate's perception of their public school education and the relation to criminal activity. Due to the nature of the equity audit, subcategories of family, community, peers, and self-reflection of prior conduct were included to offer further clarification. The subcategories of societal experiences could have a direct influence on criminal activity (see appendix C for list of questions and answers).

After reading the questionnaire answers and while conducting the focus group, several more subquestions developed and had to be clarified in the interview process. In addition to the secondary questions, categories of family, community, peers, and self were included to offer further understanding to criminal activity besides the educational experience.

1) In what ways do inmates describe how their educational experiences influenced their criminal activity?
2) What was the influence of the family?
3) What was the influence of the community?

4) What was the influence of peers?
5) What is their perception of themselves?

Table 6. Document Organization Based on Research Questions
Subquestions and Data Source

Research Question	Data Source
In what ways do inmates describe how their educational experiences influenced their criminal activity?	Questionnaire question 5–17, focus-group interviews, equity audit
What was the influence of the family?	Questionnaire question 4, focus-group interviews, equity audit
What was the influence of community?	Questionnaire questions 1–4 focus-group interviews, equity audit
What was the influence of peers?	Questionnaire questions 6, 9, 10, 12, 15, and 16, focus-group interviews, equity audit
What is their perception of themselves?	Questionnaire questions 1–3, focus-group interviews equity audit

The subcategories of the questions were purposely designed to begin with a self-reflection of early criminal activity followed by family, community, and peer influences, thus offering a possible explanation for criminal activity while in school that were the foundation for future offenses. The most prevalent answers in the early criminal activity category were drugs (both usage and distribution), theft, fighting, curfew violations, prostitution, and skipping school. The reasons for incarceration subcategory ranged from prostitution, drugs, and alcohol (usage and distribution), driving while intoxicated (DWI), evading arrest, theft, assault with deadly weapon, and violation of parole by using or selling drugs. The most interesting answers to the category of criminal activity was the reasons of *why*. We know what you did to get incarcerated and how you did it, but what are the reasons *why*. The answers were broken down into the appropriate subcategories of self, family, community, and peers. Some of the written answers are the following:

a) "I did not know that I could take my child to the hospital without insurance or money. I had to do something, and that was stealing."
b) "Drug use…addiction and knowing only one way to live."
c) "I was trying to return the items for a girlfriend and got caught."
d) "Bad lifestyle—influence from my friends."
e) "Because of the rush I got from stealing."
f) "I had a drug problem, and when I take certain drugs, it makes me do things I shouldn't."
g) "Because I had been up for many days and could not think straight."
h) "I wanted to have a family and did not want to be alone."
i) "I think the reason why I was getting high was to feel more accepted within my own skin. Also, I like to party and the feeling drugs gave me and made me feel really excited, hyped up, and fun."

j) "Because I am an addict and was trying to self-medicate in order to numb my feelings to hide the pain I was dealing with."

The answers gave us an insight that drugs had a role in criminal activity, but never answered the reason of *why* they got involved with drugs. The focus group and individual interviews expand on the why factor. The next subcategory was the demographics of the community, ranging from the family, income, community, and religious participation. The reason for this question was to determine if there was any relation between criminal activity and the demographics of the community. The majority of responses indicated that there was, in some incidences, a complete family structure, but most of the individuals came from a large and a broken dysfunctional family organization. Either the father or mother had passed away, on drugs, gang members, or were incarcerated. The majority of the responses indicated that they lived in a drug and gang zones, and the community was considered inner city. There was a church involvement, especially with the grandmothers, and one individual indicated that her father was a preacher. Most of the individuals stated that they lived in low-income communities that were "infested with gangs."

By identifying the self and community demographics as a source for criminal activity, the next series related to the primary research question category of the public school experience. The first primary research questions asked in the public school category was at what grade did they drop out of school and what was the reason. The average drop-out grade was 9.4, and the answers had several different explanations. The purpose of this question was to address the possible school conditions and the relation that caused the individual to pursue other activities. These questions also further developed the subcategory of early criminal behavior while in school, along with family, community, and peer interactions.

a) "I had to move out of the house and could not stay in school because I had to work to pay for my rent of my own place. I was an honor student and took AP classes, but was overwhelmed when I left home."
b) "Because of drugs."
c) "I had no incentive to stay. My boyfriend already graduated."
d) "I got married."
e) "Running the streets and had to find different ways to make money."
f) "My father was murdered and no mother."
g) "I had a baby."
h) "Bored."

The responses started to develop common themes as to why one dropped out of school and recorded in the appropriate codes of process, axial, and emotion. The most common answers were boredom, drugs, dysfunctional family, and pregnancies. But still the answers did not support the original research question and did not address the reason of why they were bored or why they got pregnant. The next segment of the public school experience were the positive interactions. What were some of the positive experiences you had in the public school system? The answers had mixed reviews, ranging from being a cheerleader, active in athletics and the theater, some of the teachers, to "None, and I am not sure," "I skipped a lot."

Other answers referred to liking school, but after getting involved with drugs, the experiences became negatives. The next series of questions referred to the subjects they liked and disliked in school. What was your favorite subject and why? The most favorable subjects were English, reading, math, and social studies. English because it was easy and made good grades and reading because she loved to read. Math was favored by some because of the need to count money and that they got good grades. Social Studies was favored because "it tells you the real stuff." One student favored two classes. "I enjoyed most sciences; my favorite was Biology II. It was an honors class, so it kept me interested and was more challenging. I also liked Latin II. Although it is considered to be a dead language, I have read that it is still used, especially in the medical field." The theme that is beginning to develop is the positive sense of accomplishment. "I made good grades."

What was your least favorite subject in school and why? Math was the most disliked subject from the responses. The reason ranges from "I can't understand it" to "Math—I was slower at learning than other students, and the teacher did not help me." Social studies made the list due to the boredom factor. Chemistry made the list, not because of the subject matter but due to the teacher. "I had a teacher that was not interested in teaching. She repeatedly told us that she would not answer questions and not to bother because she was pregnant and didn't feel good." Motivational themes, both positive and negative, were being developed to understand the influence that education has on the individual. "What kind of problems or negative experiences did you encounter that you did not expect?" This question was asked to determine if there were unexpected themes of occurrences that directly affected the educational experience. Only two of the responses had direct relation with their teachers. "My Spanish, geometry, Latin II, and chemistry teachers all let their personal lives disrupt their ability to teach, and we were not held accountable, at least as far as I could tell. It made learning hard for me as I had to teach myself. That is okay in college but not in high school."

The most commented unexpected situations were bad influences and bullies in school. Being picked on and not getting support from teachers and the administration was another unexpected experience. The greatest unexpected situations came from the family and community (e.g., parents getting divorced or murdered). Moving to several different schools made it difficult to have a consistent structure of stability, as well as having a baby at a young age and the negative attitudes of the other students. Gangs and drugs were a constant influence in school, and when they encountered those situations, the reaction from the inmates was that they were surprised because they thought school was a safe zone, especially in the lower grades.

What were your perceptions of other students' initial reaction to you, and did that lead to your mindset of how you should react to school? This question is a continuation of the category of peer interactions. The answers reflect a lack of interpersonal communication skills that directly affect positive or negative interactions within the community and especially within the school experience. The lack of self-esteem seems to be an important factor in the relations with other students. "I was usually talked about because of my clothes" or I "tried to keep up with the crowd" were typical answers to the question. Because of the lack of perceived acceptance, several of the students did not want to go to school. The one answer that sums up a solution to the cause and effect of the situation was that the student felt she should have acted better and that she has to take some of the responsibility for her actions.

The next category of the questionnaire was the support that the public school gave students both academically and socially. Academically, "seldom" and "never" were the majority of the answers given by students to this question. They felt that teachers only helped when they wanted to and that there was no motivation for them to help. Bullying was a big concern, and the perception was that the school did not believe it was happening. If a social situation occurred, the school never or seldom helped or offered advice. One girl stated that she got pregnant in the eighth grade, and no one offer guidance or support. One student stopped going to school for depression. She mentioned that all the school wanted to only know why she was depressed but offered no help. Another student mentioned that she got kicked off the cheerleading squad for something she did outside of school. One teacher was really concerned about the abuse of a father but offered no guidance or direction as to what to do next. Her feelings were that he just did not want to get involved.

There were positive interactions with the teachers and administration. One incident occurred when the school had a voluntary class to help the homeless. The student mentioned that that experience helped her look at life differently. Most of the responses to the question of positive collaboration between school officials were negative and only when special help was needed. The general response was that they seldom got it. The majority of positive interactions occurred between kindergarten and fourth grade and became more negative in middle and high school. The category of student interactions had both positive and negative responses. The positive were group projects and extra-curricular activities. Athletics was important for a few of the women, and that was a positive experience. Unfortunately, the negative experiences were more prominent in the responses. Drugs and gangs had a tremendous influence that developed negative responses. Being bullied and picked on were common responses, and that led to individuals being more introverted or more aggressive and mean. The extra-curricular activities are important aspects of developing organizational skills and self-esteem. Conversations with students who have participated in extracurricular activities confirm that those activities kept them out of trouble and forced them to be more organized. Unfortunately, the majority of respondents said they were not involved with extracurricular activities. The responses indicate no support from parents or from other classmates. Their extracurricular activities revolved around gangs and drug activity. The follow-up comments speak volumes about the thought process and mindset of the individuals and their educational experiences. I am submitting those comments to support the research question and subquestions to the questionnaire.

Follow-up comments by students:

a) "My whole life was a mess, starting as a kid, as early as six years old. I moved around a lot due to my mother's drug addiction. Missed a lot of schooling, but somewhere I learned to read, and I thank God for that."

b) "The ladies in the office always called the man who raised me when I went to them about the abuse at home, which always cause more abuse once I got home from school."

c) "I need my GED. I am trying really hard 'cause back then I didn't even try. No one told me why I needed an education, and the school just passed me on."

d) "Ultimately, I left school in my senior year. I dropped out because I was over worked. I felt that I never had time to be a kid, develop who I was, find hobbies, etc. I was always in the most advanced classes my school offered, in after-school programs, church, or work. There was no time for me. My grandmother tried to be my mother. My mother was more focused on her career and personal goals. There was always a lot of tension in the house, and I felt I didn't have any support. Like I said, my grandmother tried, but she wasn't my mother. My grandmother was born in 1920 and just could not relate to me and what I was going through. My school never realized what I was also going through either."

e) "I hated school, but I really wanted to like it. I was like the picture of the shark fin and goldfish you showed in class. I was bold on the top like the shark fin but a scared goldfish on the bottom. I couldn't show anyone how much I needed help. If I did, I would have shown signs of weakness. I wish someone would have been there to help me overcome my feelings of insecurity. I wish someone would have told me about the importance of education and how it could get me out of the mess that I am in. I wish I had someone who I could talk to and not make me feel like a criminal. I wish I had someone who would just listen to me and not judge me." (Note: This student came up to me after the focus-group session and asked to have her questionnaire back so she could add a final comment.)

The structured questionnaire offered an insight as to the direction for further clarification of the research question. What are the perceptions of inmates of their educational experiences in the public school educational system and the influence it had on their criminal activity? The results from the male and female participants were similar with no apparent differences in opinion. The questionnaire also developed subquestions pertaining to the family, demographics of the community, peer relations, and self-reflection. The responses made it possible to develop "unstructured" structured conversation in the focus-group discussions and the interview sessions.

Focus Group

The focus-group discussion was held in September of 2018 in the program room of the Davidson County Sheriff's Office jail facility. There were fourteen female participants, eight white and six black individuals. Eleven of the group are presently members of my purpose- and value-driven HiSET class who are seeking a high school diploma. Three were individuals that had asked to participate out of curiosity and thought they could offer additional insight to the relation between education and criminal activity. The session started at 8:00 a.m. and finished at 9:45 a.m. I am extremely grateful to these individuals who openly wanted to contribute their thoughts and possibly offer a solution to the problem by telling me their experiences. All the participants volunteered for this session and were told that they could leave at any time they felt the discussion was not beneficial, or they felt uncomfortable answering the questions. All the participants stayed for the entire session, and several asked if there would be more discussions. The session was recorded and transcribed for accuracy, and the responses were reviewed by the participants to verify the results.

The names of the participants were not used for security and confidentiality reasons and are listed as P1, P2, etc. The names are on file with the researcher and are confidential. The entire focus-group transcript is included in this research with no sections omitted. The focus group was designed to follow up on the answers from the questionnaire and to offer further clarification and theme development. The in vivo transcript was coded using additional process or action coding, and axial coding was used to relate concepts to one other. Categories were developed to offer insight as to the emotional mindset, values, and versus mentality in the relation to the research question. The first series of questions was to introduce the individuals to one another in an attempt to develop solidarity and a sense of commonality that they were not alone with their answers.

> Tom. What I'd like to do now is welcome you here to this program and remind you that this discussion is voluntary. If at any time you want to leave or feel uncomfortable about the responses, you may do so. I also want to emphasize that you're going to have a tremendous impact on the lives of many people. Before we start the questions, because we have so many people here, I'd like—if you don't mind going around the room—for you to introduce yourself and tell us where you're from and something a little bit about yourself.

The participants went around the room introducing themselves and telling the group where they were from and something about themselves; some even told us the crime they committed that got them incarcerated. The purpose to include these fourteen responses was to record the demographics of the group. Twelve of the participants are from Davison County and attended school in Nashville. One individual came from a rural area of Tennessee, and another came from Texas. All the individuals committed crimes in Davidson County. Twelve of the women have children. One individual has nine while the average seems to be two. The crimes committed are primarily drug related and armed robbery. These answers correspond to the answer given in the questionnaire and help clarify the subcategory of demographics as a theme.

P1. I'm from Nashville, Tenessee. What do you want to know about me?

Tom. What do you like doing?

P1. Drugs, unfortunately. It's the truth.

Tom. We've got to change that.

P1. I know. That's why I'm sitting here.

Tom. Good.

P2. I'm from Nashville. Davidson County.

Tom. You're from Davidson. Where'd you go to school?

P2. Hunters Lane

Tom. Did you like it?

P2. No, I dropped out. I lost my father. He was murdered. My mother passed away a couple months after that, and my granny passed away two days after my mama. So it kinda hit me really hard.

Tom. So you had a rough time adjusting?

P2. Ya, cuz I was put in the state's custody and transferred from placement to placement. So they actually put me in state's custody, so I was bounced around from placement to placement. I didn't go to real schools. It was like the education department within the facilities.

Tom. Okay. We're going to get back to that.

P3. My name is _____. I'm from Dickson, Tennessee. I have two kids, a boy and a girl.

P4. My name is _____. I'm from Mount Juliet, Tennessee. My mom passed away when I was twenty years old. I was in rehab for the first time about a month after my high school graduation. Um, I wish that they would have taught more about the effects of drugs and alcohol on your life when I was in school.

Tom. Okay, good. I'm glad you mentioned that. I'm going to come back to that.

P5. My name is _____. I'm from Antioch, Tennessee.

Tom. What was your favorite subject?

P5. Um, PE.

(*Laughter*)

Tom. Mine too. Mine too.

P6. Um, I'm _____. I'm from Nashville, Tennessee.

Tom. Where'd you go to school?

P6. I went to McGavock High School. And I have four kids.

Tom. I've heard good things about that school.

P6. About McGavock?

Tom. Yes, and I've heard some questionable things too, but I've heard some good things.

P6. It was okay… I guess.

P7. I'm ____, and I went to Whites Creek High. I'm trying to work toward my GED.

P8. I'm ____. I'm from Nashville, Tennessee.

Tom. ____, where?

P8. East Nashville.

Tom. East Nashville. I did a study on East Nashville. There's a lot of crime there. My question: is that because of school, community, family, or whatever?

All. Community.

Tom. Ya, probably.

P9. Hi, my name is ____. Um, I was actually born in Mississippi, but I was raised in Nashville. I have nine children. Um, I went to various schools due to my mother's drug dependence and me being moved around from family to family. But what I found interesting in the schools is that there was not enough outreach for children that were in trouble.

Tom. Good, I'm going to get back to that.

P10. My name is ____. I was born and raised three blocks from here, next to Glencliff. I have a son that just started the seventh grade. And I have a big problem with the schools right now.

Tom. We'll get back to that.

P11. I'm ____. I was born and raised in Texas. I just moved out here a couple years ago.

Tom. Texas is a good place to grow up.

P12. I'm from Davidson County. I have one daughter.

P13. My name is ____. I'm from Nashville, Tennessee—Davidson County. I was kicked out of all my schools by my ninth-grade year, so I went to Cheatham County for High School.

P14. My name is ____. I have two kids.

Tom. Well, it's a pleasure getting to know a little about each and every one of you, and hopefully we'll get to know one another more. Because what we're going to be doing is becoming a support group for one another. For the people who have filled out this questionnaire—and I'll get you more questionnaires for the people who just arrived—some of the questions that were asked is, if an academic problem occurred, did your school support you, firstly inside school and then outside of school? The amazing thing is most of the people said seldom or never. What problems did you have academically in school where you felt you did not get the support? Help me.

The introductory segment of the focus group explained process and interactions between criminal activities and incarceration develop categories of values and emotion. Values relate to their children and the hope that they will not follow them into jail. The emotion refers to the causes of frustration not only with the school system but of family circumstances and drug-related activities. Another important aspect of this introductory procedure was to develop a support group for each other and that they were not alone in their answers. The next question asked was pertaining to academic problems and the support you received from the school. The responses varied from little to no support to yes, if I took the initiative to ask for help.

This segment started to develop the us-versus-them mentality, but also includes the emotional category of nonacceptance by the school and the duress of pregnancy at a young age. The answers are a composite of other individuals' responses, indicating that there was little to no support for the students who got into trouble or needed assistance. These answers further support the importance of working together when there is a sense of urgency to collaboratively come up with a solution.

> **P9**. I feel like I didn't get support because nobody really checked to see—I don't know was going on. But nobody would keep up with the students. They weren't able to keep up with the students. When you have a student that leaves and comes back, and leaves and comes back three or four times in one year, that's a red flag that something's going on with the student. Guidance counselors were in place when I was in school, but they did not follow through. There were no resources. There was no, "Do you need help?" or "Is there any way I can help you in your family?" or "What's going on with you?" None of that. And when I found out I was pregnant, I was sixteen, and I was at J. T. Moore, and I went through that by myself. And I got sick at school, and that's how I found out I was pregnant by telling another girl who was pregnant what had happened. But at this point, I was going to stay in custody, and the counselors had a stigma already on me because I'm going to stay in custody—it wasn't my fault that I was there. I wasn't a bad kid. I did not have behavioral problems. I just didn't have nobody to raise me.

In a private conversation after the focus-group meeting, I asked why she got pregnant, and her answer was, "He said he loved me, and no one ever told me that before."

The next response offered clarification as to why they were in school and the importance of having an education. The following exchange exemplifies the frustration that several of the students have with their public school education.

> **P7**. When I was in school, they just wanted you to work. They just handed you work and said do this—that's when I was in school, and I'm thirty-four.
> **Tom**. What was the purpose of them just handing you work?
> **P7**. Um, I don't know. Cuz I didn't do it.
> **Tom**. Let me ask you another question—
> **P7**. You know you could walk out of class, and they wouldn't try to stop you.
> **Tom**. _____, let me ask you another question. Did they explain to you why you had to study math?
> **P7**. No.
> **Tom**. Or why you had to study history? Anybody else? Help me.
> **All**. No.
> **Tom**. So basically everyone is saying no.

P14. Our teacher says that we're going to have to use it whenever we get older, but I never really saw that being practical because I'm not going to be a scientist.

Tom. I understand that.

P10. It was my understanding that we had to have so many assignments turned in to figure out grade averages. We had to do so many so that they would have the number of grades for their books. That's what I was told.

Tom. That's a good answer. But is it still adequate for answering the question of why you had to study?

All. No.

Tom. This is the one area we want to change. Anyone else want to throw more comments in about the academic help from the schools?

The answers to this question of academic assistance and purpose of education is starting to develop a theme of lack of support or knowledge of the reasons for an education. The following questions are based on the children of the focus-group members. The average age of this group is thirty-three, and as stated before, twelve of the members have children who are in school. The purpose is to see if there is a relation between when they attended school and what is currently happening now with their children. The question is based on what the experiences of your children in the public school system are and how it affects them. I felt it was important to include this information due to the fact that many of the participants have been out of school for several years.

P10. Based on what our kids are going through right now?

Tom. Sure.

P10. My son struggles in school. So he comes home with math work and with some grammar stuff, and he sits down, and he just stares at it—he has no clue what's going on. And I'm asking him, "Did your teacher not go over any of this? How can you not know what to do right now?" And he's like, "I don't know." So I don't know if it's just that he spaces out or if it's the teacher. Because the teacher said she's done what she's supposed to do, and he says that she doesn't—so I don't know.

Tom. What about you?

P13. My grandson, um, turned eight years old yesterday. And I think it's really shitty that our kids now are not taught how to even [interact] like this. They don't learn nothing but computers. He does his homework on computers. He does everything on computers. Okay, what's going to happen when the computer crashes? He's not going to know how to do a damn thing. They don't have home economics in school, so they don't learn how to cook or sew or do anything anymore. They don't even know how to write in cursive anymore.

(Responses of agreement)

Tom. What were you saying?

P7. It's right. They don't even teach my daughter how to write in cursive no more.

P9. My son's in eighth grade. When he was in seventh grade, I wrote a letter to him in cursive from jail, and he said he couldn't read it because he didn't know how to read cursive. And I said, "Do you not know how to write it?" He don't know how to write in cursive. He don't know how to read in cursive. I'm thrown off by that because I don't understand how my child don't know cursive. That is a part of the education system.

P13. And they do their math with calculators now.

P9. Everything is done with calculators, and with the laptops at the school.

Tom. You said they're now using calculators.

P13. That's right. How are they going to do math unless it's with a calculator?

P7. And they just pass them, no matter what.

The answers provided offered an insight as to what is happening now in our public school inner city. The general consensus is that the material taught is not relevant to meet the needs and that critical-thinking skills are not encouraged. They believe that students today are taught to be dependent on the use of calculators and computers to find the answers to a question and not the use of logic to determine an answer. The next series of questions pertained to their children's actual knowledge of the subjects and the school's attitude to just pass them on to the next grade.

> **P10**. My son is in the seventh grade, and he should be in the sixth grade. That child did not pass the sixth grade. I had a meeting with the teachers. They told me he's not ready to go, but we got to send him on. Why do we have to send him on? He's going to be behind in every year going up now.
>
> **Tom**. What other examples do you have personally gone through where you and your children had problems academically and sought support but never got it?
>
> **P9**. I'm _____. Just this past school year, my son Isaiah (*pseudonym*) who's in the fifth grade came home with simple division, basic first division. My son did not know how to do that. And I asked, "Isaiah, how is it that you don't know how to do this? Do you not know your multiplication tables?" He barely knew his multiplication tables. Okay, I talked to the school. I talked to his math teacher. His math teacher, her excuse was, "We're working with the students right now—but we're almost at the end of the school year" (at that point). Coming to the end of the school year before I came to jail, school got out the week before I came to jail. They send you these reports home, and Isaiah was like two or three points from failing. And I went to the school and had a meeting with the teachers. The day I set the meeting up, I had to go to another meeting for some personal stuff, but the same day, I went to school. She told me that she talked to Isaiah and said everything was okay, and I said, "No, everything is not okay. He is not meeting the requirements to go to the sixth grade. Do not pass him." She said, "Well, it's only by one point, and he's going to do this math packet for me." And she passed him anyway. Let's keep in mind that she passed my son, but she did not set up anything for him to do summer school. They didn't send any papers home for me to sign him up for summer school. They just passed my children. And at the school in the inner city, primarily, they're passing our kids. They're half-teaching them and passing them. My son that's at Buena

Vista, he's in the second grade. I'll tell you what they're doing up there—they don't even teach math. They don't even have a math teacher this year. They are behind with children and reading up there, so they quit reading this year. Everybody got high points in reading, and none of the other stuff was pushed, and I did not like that.

P13. My granddaughter was going to the magnet school over there in East Nashville. Um, she was in the fourth grade, and we had to go to a parent conference, and she was only reading on a second-grade level. They hadn't even started doing times tables. She couldn't do any of that, and they passed her to the fifth grade. And because they passed her, we couldn't even get her any type of summer school.

P10: They don't offer summer school anymore.

P4. It's because nobody's stepping out. My niece she was so embarrassed because they didn't teach her, and she's dyslexic. They would call on her, and she would get so embarrassed because she was dyslexic, and she'd read backward. But they never worked with her. They never put her in special education classes to try to help her, so she dropped out and joined a gang. Because that where she felt, you know, she was accepted.

The stories that are being told lead to further categories of rejection, gang acceptance and affiliation, attitudes (both student and teacher), expectations or lack thereof, embarrassment (direct link to attitudes), and perceptions of reality. The answers refer to their experiences and their children, indicating that conditions have not changed in the school system. What was prevalent then is relevant now. The following questions pertain to the support the school gave you or your children in making decisions, which further develops the category of values.

Tom. If a social problem occurred in school, what type of support did you get from the school district to assist you? Because it's going back to the comment that we made earlier. You're on the fence. You've got a decision to make. How much pain is going to cost? Did they ever guide you in that aspect to say, "Listen, you've got a decision to make"?

P9. I don't think in the social part of schooling. School starts at nine. My son will leave at seven thirty or eight o'clock. They like to talk and stuff before school, you know, cuz they don't even let the kids in the school building before nine o'clock. So my son stopped going. He stopped leaving early in the morning, and I said, "How come you're not leaving early like you used to?" Now he'll leave like ten minutes 'til nine, so he can get breakfast at school, you know. So I'm like, "Why you not going?" He said, "Mama, I don't want to go." He said, because these other children are recruiting our children to be in gangs.

Tom. Got it. What experiences have you had socially? Did the school help you or not?

P5. No. You mean me personally?

Tom. Yep.

P5. No.

Tom. Or do you know of a story of other people who wanted help but never got it?

P5. Not really.

Tom. Anybody else? To me, this is a big problem.

P9. Ya, the whole system is a big problem.

The interesting aspect of this question is that there are different view or perceptions of reality. Some indicate that there is a big problem with the assistance that schools offer and other participants say *no*. The next series of questions focus on the importance of family involvement or the lack thereof and will develop more categories and themes.

Tom. All right, let me go on then. What about family? What about your personal family? What kind of family structure did you have? Let's just go right around the room. Did you grow up in a family with a mother and a father?

P1. My grandparents.

Tom. I'm sorry, but could be a great alternative?

P1. My grandparents raised me, and I was fortunate.

Tom. Her grandparents raised her. What about someone else?

P2. They did up until the age of fifteen when I lost my parents.

Tom. When you lost your dad?

P2. Yep.

Tom. Then who took care of you?

P2. They wouldn't place me. That's the thing, they put me back in the system. They were like…nobody wanted to take me cuz they didn't give my grandmother the opportunity to take me.

P3. Um, dysfunctional family until that led me to state's custody, when I was fourteen.

Tom. State custody at fourteen?

P4. I did up until the fifth grade. My parents got divorced because of my father's alcoholism. Then he kinda disappeared, but my mom was a single mom raising two kids.

Tom. ____?

P8. You said, did I grow up with my mother and daddy?

Tom. Yes. Who'd you grow up with?

P8. One parent.

Tom. What parent? Your mom?

P8. Yes.

Tom. ____?

P5. I had both my parents.

Tom. Both parents?

P6. I had both my parents. I grew up with both my parents. And all their children graduated high school.

Tom. So your brothers and sisters graduated high school too?

P6. Mmmm.

Tom. I'm going to get back to that in a minute.

P7. I grew up with both my parents. And all my kids haven't graduated yet.

Tom. Both parents?

P9. Um, I grew up for a little while with my mother until her drug problem got out of hand, and then I was moved from my biological aunt to a friend of the family, and that went on for many, many years until finally I decided to call DCS because I was tired of moving around. And I went into state's custody at like fifteen.

Tom. Okay.

P10. Um, I was raised by my grandmother until I was fifteen and became a ward of the state.

P12. Both my parents and my grandparents.

Tom. We're going to get back to that.

P11. I had both parents.

Tom. You had both parents?

P13. I was raised by my father. He was an alcoholic and a truck driver.

Tom. That's a rough life.

P14. My parents divorced when I was four because of drug use, and we lived with my grandparents. My mom remarried when I was twelve. My mom just really paid the bills, and my grandmother raised me.

Tom. Parenting is so important. Is there a correlation between being incarcerated and being raised by a one-parent family?

(*Some said no. Some said there could be.*)

Tom. Okay, P8 says no. P10 says possibly, or absolutely is.

P9. I say possibly. Because there are some single parents raising some amazing kids. So maybe, could be.

There seems to be two responses to question of family. The majority of participants grew up in a dysfunctional family structure. Single parent, grandparents, or wards of the state were the typical answer. A couple of participants grew up with both parents, but still they ended up in jail. The question is why. The individuals with a two-parent structure were incarcerated due the usage and distribution if drugs. These results lead the researcher to further explore and include expectation, values, dreams, and goals. The next question relates to peer relations and the influence it had on their criminal activity.

Tom. What about the relation with other students and their influence on your criminal activity?

(*Reflective comments*)

P9. Well, um, for me, I was already just so withdrawn from life it didn't affect me because I was a loner, and I was probably one of the kids that nobody hung out with, so it didn't affect me cuz I was always by myself anyway. And I tend to gravitate toward the people who nobody wants to talk to or hand out with.

Tom. You were saying?

P6. It didn't affect me either. Other students didn't affect me either.

Tom. A lot of the people have answered bully: they were bullied, so they became isolated.

P7. I was the bully.

Tom. Oh, you were the bully?

(*Laughter*)

P7. I was the bully. I was bad. I grew up around a whole bunch of gangs. I dropped out. I was bad.

Tom. P13?

P13. I wasn't ever a bully, but I was probably more of a negative influence on people than they were to me. I had my own place. I had drugs. I had all that, so I was probably the bad influence.

Tom. What about just a general observation from your schools, whether it be the high school or grade school that you went to—your observations of the students around you? Did they support you?

P9: No. And when you brought up bullying, I didn't think of it from that standpoint. I guess I was just really bullied a lot because I didn't meet their standards. Like I didn't have the nice clothes they had, the nice shoes, or whatever. I didn't meet their standards. So you don't want to meet those kids' standards, or you don't have what they think you should have, then you are definitely the underdog, and you're definitely going to get picked on.

Tom. P1?

P1. When I was in school, you were in this certain clique, this certain clique, or this certain clique. Like, the popular kids with money or preps—we called them preps back, nice clothes, etc. Or the poor kids, which would usually leave and go get drunk or whatever. If you didn't click with them…I'd usually go out the front door and just not go back.

The answers to bullying and relations with other students led to another category of upbringing and the influence that had on one's attitude. Subconsciously, bullying had a direct relation with one's self-esteem. There seems to be a direct correlation between acceptance by one's peers and one's attitude or motive to get that acceptance. The final series directly relate to the public school experience and the influence it had on criminal activities.

Tom. What are your feelings about your public school education? Did it have an influence on your criminal activity?

P9. Yes.

Tom. You're saying yes. P9 says yes. P7 says yes. I'm saying this because the comments that you made earlier about when things went wrong within school, they didn't support you.

(*Responses in agreement*)

Tom. So could that be part of the reason why you got involved with criminal activities that led to your incarceration?

(*Responses in agreement*)

P13. I guess we were allowed to hustle, I guess, in school, cuz I got a pack of cigarettes every morning with my lunch money. I got a dollar a day, and cigarettes were ninety cents. So I had to hustle my lunch money. I mean, and it was okay back then.

TOM. That was the standard back then.

(*Laughter*)

P12. Well, I sold marijuana at school, and my parents…I was one of the kids that got everything that I could've possibly wanted. It wasn't because of my parents nor the school. I strayed off on my own. Hanging with other people that was older than me, and most of them had everything that they wanted too. Half the time it's not the parents, it's not the school—it's you.

(*Responses of agreement*)

TOM. I like that answer because it goes back to what we talked about before. You have a decision to make.

(*Responses of agreement*)

TOM. I like that, P12, that was a good comment.

P4. I agree with what she said because I was skipping school and barely going my senior year. And they called my mom at work. And then they made sure that I was there every day on time, or I was going to be expelled and kept from graduating. But I've always been a really inquisitive person, I want to know about everything. I wanted to hang out with the kids that were doing the bad things. It wasn't my mom, it wasn't the school. They both tried to, you know…

TOM. Okay. Most of you have kids. What are you going to tell them?

P12. The things that I've done, I'm going to teach my daughter that that's not the right way to go. Cuz nowadays you need an education to get most of the jobs that are available. I don't want my daughter to follow in the footsteps that I was in.

P9. And, um, you know, I had nobody to support me growing up or push education. So now with my children, I push education. I push it and push it and push it. Even though I come in and out of jail, I'm still pushing education. While I'm in jail, when I call home, I tell them you all go to school, what work did you do—you know, I'm constantly pushing education. Cuz I have boys, and I have girls, and it's important to me that they finish school and that they go to college. Now if you do that, I don't care what you do—I do, but at least you have something to fall back on.

TOM. What about this? Your child is in a problem situation. Are you going to tell them to go to the school officials?

P9. I have told them that in the past. The school officials are not going to…I have a problem with that situation too, Mr. Tom. Cuz just with my three youngest kids, I have a lot of stuff. Like with Daniel, I told him to go tell the principal or go tell the person who they have ordained is the safe person that you can talk to.

TOM. And what's their response?

P9. Um, "We're going to take care of it," or "We're going to do something." And nothing happens. One day my son had $20. One of the students took his money. He went to the safe person to keep from fighting and told them because he was upset. He didn't get his money back. They didn't try to get it back. They are not responsible to these children.

Tom. All right, tell me more.

P6. I didn't have any problems with my children in school. My daughter went to college and my kids graduated high school. And they did pretty good in school. I didn't ever have any problems.

The new category added was the children of the participants. The theme that was being developed by the individuals was that they have to be more proactive on their relationship with their children. An addition to the categories was individual responsibility for the actions that have been made. The response made by P12 sums up the solution to personal behavior that led to incarceration. "Half the time it's not the parents, it's not the school—it's you." The last question was based on a picture I placed on a PowerPoint slide, and I asked them to comment using an analogy from their own life experiences.

Tom. I'm putting a picture (*on the board*) of a side view of a shark's fin on top of the water and goldfish underneath the water. You see that? Say your name and tell me an analogy of what you think this picture means.

P4. Things aren't as bad as they always look or seem.

Tom. Good. I like this picture because it looks stormy up here, and it looks calm down here. Give me another analogy. Samantha is saying things don't look as bad as they seem.

P9. When I look at that, I think about—and still thinking about—the school system and my kids, how they have to go on with a hard exterior like the shark. But the goldfish at the bottom is the person he really is on the inside. So he has to put on that facade at the top like he's so hard and everything's okay.

P14. Because there's a storm around him, there's a defense mechanism. That's what it looks like to me. Because of the environment that's on the surface.

Tom. So it's like they have to put on a facade?

(*Responses of agreement*)

Tom. Anybody else?

(*No response*)

Tom. To me, this picture means a lot because I think you're exactly right. So many times, we as individuals have to put on this facade, yet a lot of times we're scared. We're scared, but we gotta fake it. Does anyone else have anything they want to add to this discussion about public school education having an influence on your criminal activity?

P9. I think that if I had more support in schools, it's probably a good chance that I could've went another direction. If they had taught me about the things you could become in life and told me I had these opportunities to do these things—doctors, nurses—you have these opportunities to become anything you want to be. I probably would have looked at life a little more differently.

P10. I was led by fear, I think. I did really well in school, but it wasn't because anybody was trying to push me or encourage me to be something in my life. It was because they were telling me if you don't graduate, you're not going to be able to get a job, and if you can't get a job where you going to go, because at eighteen you're on your own. I was a ward of the state. I had to have a plan.

Tom. That's a great comment. Anybody else?

(*No response*)

Tom. I want to thank you for participating in this. I'll go back and study this and write it out—and try to come up with some sort of scenario. I want to get back to you on this. Thank you.

Note: This student came up to me after the focus-group session and asked to have her questionnaire back so she could add a final comment. I included her questionnaire comment in the focus-group transcription:

I hated school, but I really wanted to like it. I was like the picture of the shark fin and goldfish you showed in class. I was bold on the top like the shark fin but a scared goldfish on the bottom. I couldn't show anyone how much I needed help. If I did, I would have shown signs of weakness. I wish someone would have been there to help me overcome my feelings of insecurity. I wish someone would have told me about the importance of education and how it could get me out of the mess that I am in. I wish I had someone who I could talk to and not make me feel like a criminal. I wish I had someone who would just listen to me and not judge me.

The focus-group session was extremely interesting in that it offered more categories of influence ranging from individual to responsibility for their children. More themes developed of insecurity and just wanting to be loved or accepted. The most important theme was that conditions have not changed since they were in school and the experiences that their children are having now. The important category that was included was upbringing and the influence that had on their criminal activity. In the next series of one-on-one interviews, the individuals were asked to further clarify *why* they got involved in criminal activities, including the use of drugs. Two candidates were selected. Their names are not included due to security and confidentiality concerns and are classified as participants P1 and P2. The first person interviewed was a thirty-seven-year-old Hispanic male on parole. He was heavily tattooed, had a weathered light-skin complexion, approximately six feet tall and 240 pounds. When I first met him, my initial reaction was, *Here is a guy one does not want to mess with.* The second person interviewed was a twenty-four-year-old African American female who was waiting to be sentenced on various charges ranging from prostitution, armed robbery, and assault with a deadly weapon. P2 is light-skinned, heavily tattooed on arms and neck, five feet three inches tall, and approximately 125 pounds—a beautiful girl but with a skeptical attitude based on her past experiences. Both interviews are transcribed in their entirety, except for two small segments that described brutal criminal activity that had no relation to the scope of this research.

Interview I

The interview was selected by reading responses from the questionnaire due to the content of the message and the descriptive nature of his answers. P1 had been incarcerated several times and had just recently been released. He was a member of a support group who participated answering the questionnaire and just wanted to help. He was a former gang member who was classified as a lieutenant in the organization. The language was descriptive, and he often used slang or coarse terminology. The interview was conducted in September of 2018 and lasted one hour forty-seven minutes. There were additional outcomes that gave clarity to the reason why and offered solutions to the problems of educational system and criminal activity.

P1 was from the Houston, Texas, area, and I wanted to see if his answers were similar to the students who attended Nashville schools. I informed P1 this was a voluntary interview that would be recorded and that I also would be taking notes. I also informed him that his answers could have a positive impact to help initiate change in the educational system. Ironically, his answer to be part of this research was a theme that developed throughout the questionnaire and focus-group sessions: the theme of the importance of inclusion or lack thereof and that, through their efforts, the participants may develop a self-actuation of importance or of being a nonfactor. The categories supporting the theme are emotion and help. When I asked P1 for his help, his reply was, "You need…you need help. You can't do it alone. You know what I mean? That's the same thing with me. I can't do this alone. I need help. It may not be at the level you need it, but I mean, it's just…that I want to help."

The significance of his remarks can be interpreted as a plea for help in that he wanted to be included in this process so he could feel he was contributing to a positive cause. He was honored that he was asked to participate, which improved his self-esteem. P1 also mentioned that he would answer the questions as best as he could, which also reenforces the categories of honesty and values. I originally included in the areas of concentration to be community, family, school, and peers; but through P1's desire to be included, I added another area of "self": the process of self-actuation of what the individual was and what the individual would like to be. In the next series of questions, I was curious as to the motivation to be involved in criminal activities. I was not concerned about what or how P1 committed crimes, but I wanted to know the *why* and how many times had he been incarcerated. I wanted to know if there was a process or pattern to his arrests that led to incarceration and recidivism into the prison system.

P1. I mean, I'll tell you anything, whatever you want to know…I'll tell you.

Tom. How many times and why?

P1. I was incarcerated three times.

Tom. *Why?*

P1. You are going to…this is going to shock you…but two times for women.

Tom. Really?

P1. The first time I went to prison, there was this girl, her name was Jessica. And, uh, she was twenty-two. I was like sixteen, seventeen, so she was rocking the cradle. So she had me sprung, she put it on me…you know, she was an older woman. I was still a teenager, so I didn't know how to act. And, uh, I went to prison for evading arrest with a motor vehicle, unauthorized use of a motor vehicle, auto theft, and retaliation. I retaliated against her because she filed charges against me. But I retaliated because it was…I retaliated because…it all comes down to influence. People around you like, man, you a hoe, you a sucker, you gonna let that bitch, man, you know what, you're right you gonna…you know…you're right…you think I'm a hoe? Where's that gun at right there? I'm gonna show you how much I'm a hoe. I can show you. Anyway, like I said, pride gets you in trouble. So I went to prison for that. I went in prison. I got locked up. I was like, damn, you know? I was a prison gang member. I was a prison gang member before I went to prison. So I was already in there with a prison gang. I wasn't in there for, "Oh, I'm scared, I'm going to join these people." No, it was from the streets. Everybody I grew up around, so we joined this family…so I didn't know…

In talking to P1, I found out that his criminal activities started at a young age, but this was the first time he was incarcerated. P1's answers developed subcategories of pride, retaliation, and outcomes, reenforcing the codes of process and emotion. The older woman took advantage of him. He did something wrong, and she filed charges. The early criminal-activity category started to develop, which included the basic crimes of evading arrest, auto theft, etc. But the addition of "retaliation" was the interesting category that needed an explanation as to why. P1's answer was influence with other individuals in the community and that pride gets one into trouble. P1 took the comments personally, and to show the gang members that they were wrong, he retaliated. This theme of peer pressure started to form and became a substantial reason for criminal activity. Categories of excitement, money, and acceptance became reasons for gang activity that became primary forms of concentration, and family and school became secondary. All these activities became a process for gang involvement and eventual incarceration. I started to realize that Maslow's hierarchy of needs could be a contributing factor in criminal activities. My next question was, "Why did you join the gang?"

> **P1.** We do it because at times, it's fun, it's exciting, it's fast money. We all believe that you are gonna die for me, and I'm gonna die for you. This is for life, bro. This this, this that—wah, wah, wah, wah, wah, wah, wah.
>
> **Tom.** They're building a foundation. The gang is building a foundation with you, "Hey, we'll take care of you."
>
> **P1.** Everybody does, exactly. That's why everybody say that we all take care of you. But the purpose of me getting in was…my purpose, my personal purpose of getting in the family that I got in was the fact that I didn't like two of the families that I had hearing about growing up. And I didn't like how they abused their own members, which are their own Mexicans. So I was like, man, you know these people, so when I started talking to one of the guys, one of the people that I run with whatever now…they were like, man, we don't roll like that, you know what I'm saying? Over here, even the leaders get their hands dirty. Leaders don't call the shots. They the ones that do the shots, you know. He goes, that's what it's about over here, you know what I'm saying? Everybody's going to eat over here, and everybody's car is going to be pulled over here. So you know, I says well, you know, that sounds brotherhood, you know (?), HBO. So we became what we became. Was it fun for a couple of years? Yeah, it was real fun.

The foundation for the hierarchy of needs was being created. "We will take care of you," implying that the gang will give him food, shelter, colors (clothing); that they will protect him and make him feel like he belonged. The gang provided excitement and money, which became a process code for interpretation as to the question *why*. P1's answer also implied that the gangs had an organizational structure of governance that provided security by establishing norms or expectations. P1 further talked about values, morals, and consequences, which added more subcategories to the research.

P1. Until, uh, until a murder happened. They killed (?)…the leader got killed. He got chopped up in pieces, and they threw him in Galveston Bay. It's on the internet if you want to look it up. That happened, before all that happened, it was love. There was so much love. We were running around three or four carloads. We had like three of four of these, two Escalades. The guy, Tiny, was selling keys…cocaine, whatever, whatever, and was taking care of everybody. For Christmas, he gave everybody a Glock 45, gun, a bottle of tequila stuff. And you know like $1,000, and these are like eighty members, so he's giving that to everybody.

The categories of belonging and acceptance were primary reasons for gang affiliation, which started to develop further themes to understand the concepts of criminal activities. The interesting aspect is that values also played a role in what type of criminal activity was acceptable. Values not only for the gang but also for P1. He liked the comradery of the gangs, especially the fun activities, but there were limits. The gang structure or governance also provided for boundaries, and if the boundaries were crossed, there were consequences.

Tom. So in other words, he's building a foundation, he's protecting you, he's giving you food, clothing. He's giving you protection, he's making you feel that you belong to the group.

P1. Yeah, it makes you feel…we feel untouchable sometimes because there's fifteen of us, twenty of us, brought in as one. There're three or four carloads, and we all rode together. When we go to a restaurant, they had to put three or four tables together. That's just the way we used to roll.

The responses to the previous questions further enforced the importance of Maslow's hierarchy of needs by making P1 feel he belonged, appreciated, and accepted, which the third portion of the pyramid and a process code for affiliation represents. The next series of questions pertained to his family. I expected to have a conversation about his direct family, but his answers were still in tuned to the importance of the gang. Family to P1 meant gang affiliation.

P1. You know that helped me a lot. And you know when I tell you…when I went to prison, it even helped me how to read and write Spanish. You know, 'cause you got the homeboy right there So you're sitting here trying to read, and I guess since I'm Hispanic or Mexican, it's in my nature. It's not hard for me to roll my tongue, so whatever, whatnot…so I started reading and learning, and yeah, you know, being a leader on different prisons. I was a lieutenant, and I would make sure I would have to fix problems for the family, make sure they didn't escalate, make sure there were no killings, stabbings going on. The guards disrespect one of my members—you know we talk to them because they can get hit too.

The importance of the gang led to his survival in prison, and family meant gang. The "gang family" provided education, and as he developed respect, he became a leader by becoming a fix-it person. If a problem occurred, he felt it was his responsibility to handle the situation. He became important, and he started to develop a sense of self-esteem by being considered to be an important person. Another code being developed was the us-versus-them mentality. This mindset could be a reason for his rejection of authority, which could have been established in his younger days in the public school system. Those questions and answers are explored later on in the interview. The next question was about his upbringing and his biological family. I was trying to establish if the hierarchy of needs was relevant in the family structure.

Tom. What was your family like? What was the family structure?
P1. At home?
Tom. Yeah, at home—your family, your mom and dad.
P1. At home, we were good.
Tom. So they gave you a place to stay, they gave you food and shelter…
P1. We were good. We were good. My family was good. My dad was good. My mom was good. You know, we were all good. But my brother, they were older, and you know, he went his way, and little brother always wants to be like a big brother. You know big brother was a Crip and whatnot [an item that has something in common that has already been named], so I wanted to be a Crip, and that's how the gang life whatnot came about.

I could not get a solid answer to the foundation of the family, but the importance of peer pressure and influenced played a major role in P1's development. He mentioned that his parents were good, but the influence on his way of life came from his older brothers. One brother was a Crip (gang name), so P1 wanted to become a Crip. The category added was role model. I asked P1 to tell me more about his homelife, and that is when he mentioned the environment that he was living in and how that had an impact on his life.

P1. My mom was good to me. My dad was good to me. We lived in an area, that's why I say it has a lot to do with the areas we grew up in. It's easy to get caught up in it, and it's not. When I was born until I was eleven or twelve years old, we lived in Northwest Houston, Spring Branch. A neighborhood called Spring Branch. We were good, man. School and everything. I remember I used to always say I wanted to be a firefighter. I used to always tell my dad, "Look, Dad, look. That's going to be me driving that red truck—you know, the firetruck."

The interesting aspect was that P1 had a relationship with his father and said he was a good man, and his mother was good too. He even had dreams of becoming a fireman and wanted to drive the big red firetruck. He even liked school. The categories of dreams and goals were part of his upbringing. P1 admitted that the area he was brought up in had a direct positive relation to his thought process. But that all changed when they had to move into Section 8 housing in an area called the *Hole*.

P1. When we moved over here to the Hole, it's called the Hole, it's only one way in, one way out, 75 percent black, 25 percent Hispanic. When we moved over here to housing whatever, Section 8 whatever, all my family lived there.

My aunts, my mom's sisters, and all them. All my uncles been in prison. You know a lot of my uncles have been in prison too. All my family's been in prison. All the way from my mom's brothers and whatnot. So that's that. And we move over there. And that's where you're wrecking on weed, crack, and this and that and everything, and then from there, you just decide to say, "Fuck school."

The category of demographics developed into understanding of *why* there was criminal activity due to low income, drugs, racial tensions, peer pressure, machismos masculinities, and dysfunctional families. The theme from P1's experiences is survival on a daily basis with no positive expectations for the future. With all that pressure to survive, P1 developed a negative attitude toward school. The question is, what did the school do to assist P1 in developing a positive attitude toward school and himself? The next section of questioning pertains to his educational experiences.

> **Tom.** All right, let's go on to…what was your education? What was schooling like? Grade school, high school—how far did you go?
> **P1.** I made it to the sixth grade.
> **Tom.** Okay, what was that like? What was you experience like in school?
> **P1.** I didn't really have…I can't say I had an experience at school. And the reason I say I didn't really have an experience at school because…I would tell them to go the other way. They want to go, but I don't know which way they are trying to go…so I got confused and said to hell with it. Anyway, okay, sorry about that. I don't think I had a school education. I can't say I did. Did I remember going to school? Yes. Do I remember doing homework? No. Do I remember reading a report card? No.

What were the expectations that the school placed on P1, and did they explain the importance of an education? The category of value or importance of education was not fully explained. P1 became confused and gave up. His attitude was wrong because he did not ask for further clarification, but the school was also wrong in not pursuing to clarify and help P1. His attitude also got him suspended from school, and he was sent to another institution on the other side of the city. The miscommunication category between P1 and the school further developed behavior problems. These decisions further enhanced the category of us-versus-them mentality and apathy over empathy.

> **P1.** Some kind of academy place. I can't remember what it was. Well, when I went to that academy place in Southwest Houston, I'm from the Northside. The school sent me over there. How am I supposed to get over there? I'm a fifteen-year-old kid. So I buy a low-rider car. So now I got a low-rider car, I'm fifteen/sixteen, I'm going to the Southside. This is when the Northside don't like the Southside. The Southside didn't like the Northside. So it's like what's going on? And then it's like, I used that to meet more people, and every night I would steal stuff and load my car up with so much electronics, go to school in the morning, and everybody's buying them. So I went to school to sell electronics, not to learn.

The transfer to another school has many manifolds of consequences and actually caused more problems. This action code further enhanced the versus code. The original school was not prepared to handle P1, or they just did not want to face the problem and take on the responsibility, or they just did not care. P1's attitude was that the old school just did not want to "put up with me." The complications of sending him to another school, especially into a culture of conflict and competition, caused P1 to further distance himself from the importance of education. This transfer of schools caused P1 to further reach out to criminal activity for the purpose of survival.

TOM. Did the schools offer you any help?

P1. I can't say it did, or it didn't. I mean, whatever the school does…I don't know 'cause it didn't affect me. I was going to do my thing, not their thing.

TOM. Did they try to teach you values…and tell you that what you are doing is wrong?

P1. No, you know what? These schools are not like Brentwood schools, Franklin schools. You know when you've got low-income schools and public schools and whatnot, it's different…because the teacher knows—oh, you just want to fuck that girl, get out of my class, get out of my class, get out of my class. All you want to do is be back there and flirt with her. I'm going to get you out of my class. But I'm scheduled to be in that class. But I'm not going in there for that class. Yeah, it's on my schedule, but I'm going in there for her. You know, so they know that and instead of trying to teach you wrong from right, they tell you to get out of the class. That's just the schools that we went to, that I went to that were like that.

TOM. That was the attitude…

P1. Yes, the attitude you have…directly reflects the attitude that the teachers have toward you.

TOM. So the teachers didn't really offer much help.

P1. Naw.

P1's remarks further developed the codes of action and versus by comparing suburban schools to the inner city. That the different school settings had a different mindset as to the importance of education. The values category was further explained in that he had different values due to his different culture. These values affected him with the school, as well as with other students. Another category that must be included is an individual being stereotyped due to attitude and possibly a cultural background. P1 is Hispanic, and he attended a primarily an African American school. The perception of apathy was prevalent in P1's mindset in that he felt the teachers did not care and just want him out of the classroom. I wanted to pursue this thought process, and I asked about his academic achievement in the first grade.

TOM. What about…when you were in first grade? Did you pass first grade, or did they just promote you, just pass you on?

P1. I think they just passed me on, to be honest.

TOM. All the way up to sixth grade?

P1. I think so. I mean, my mom could probably tell you more about that because me personally, I can't remember it, and I didn't care if I flunked or failed.

Failed or passed. And I don't even remember...I don't even remember. I failed the sixth grade, I believe. I think that's why I didn't go on to the seventh, and...but I mean, I really did...at school...

The apparent attitude of the school was to just pass P1 on and let another teacher deal with the problems. This attitude could be considered the Pontius Pilate approach to students. Wash your hands and pass the student on to the next teacher. This axial coding was important to determine the interactions and attitudes of teachers toward the student. The process of passing the student to the next grade was expedient for the school but had detrimental effects on P1 and the other participants in this study. This claim is supported by the equity audit of grade school equivalency as reported in the beginning of this chapter. P1's comments also indicated a poor attitude on his part, further developing the emotion and attitude categories. His attitude could also be interpreted as a lack of motivation that was not supplied by the school. The next series of questions related to a sense of purpose, norms, goals, and dreams.

> TOM. Did they ever give you or tell you or give you a sense of purpose, or have you set goals or dreams?
>
> P1. At school?
>
> TOM. Yeah.
>
> P1. At school...where I was going to school, that area, that side of town, Northwest Houston, I mean Northeast Huston off Mason Tidwell, it was called Kirby Middle School. It's not...that school right there, they popped you for being in late. Pow, pow. Now just with that...that did it to me. If my mom allowed these people to hit me, then me and mom got problems. Now the dude that just hit me, we definitely got problems. So you know what, fuck you and your school. I'm going to skip school and every day I'm going to check the mail, and if somebody from the school is writing, I'm going to cut 'em up and throw 'em away.

The attitudes that P1 have acquired could have a direct relation between the way teachers interact with the students and behavioral problems. The way teachers treat students could be the reason why P1 treated others in a similar manner. The interactions became linear instead of transactional forms of communication. Linear is very dictatorial and caused resentment and possible retaliation in the mindset of P1. I wanted to further pursue the hierarchy of needs in relation to P1's education and criminal activity.

> TOM. So in other words, the school...did they give you a safe place to go? Was it safe in school?
>
> P1. Was it safe in school? No. We all had bandanas everywhere.
>
> TOM. Got it.
>
> P1. It was like Julio—the Gangsta Paradise. Now it wasn't as bad or whatnot, but that's what you get. You know you got little Crips, little kids...we all think we are tough little gang members or whatnot, I mean.
>
> TOM. So in other words, yeah, the gangs gave you a structure, but did the school give you a structure by giving you food—breakfast or lunch or something?

And did the administration and teachers ever really give you protection and that they made you feel safe and that you belonged to that school?

P1. No, I mean, just the opposite. Anywhere you…I mean, schools like that, they are going to…they are not going…I mean, it's like you, it's like everywhere else. But the majority of the teachers there, if they know you are only there for this or that, and you are steady walking around with your pants down, they are not going to waste their time on you. So them, they have a big point because no matter how I dress, how I look, what I'm trying to do to that girl in that classroom, your [teachers] job is to imprint it in my brain to learn to do this or do that. No, you kick me out. No, you do this, you do that, you do this, you do that. It is my way or the highway.

I was trying to find a relation between P1's experiences and a foundation of security and trust between him and the school. The axial code responses became a theme that developed between the negative interactions of teachers toward their students and further enhanced the category of us-versus-them mentality. In addition to the apparent negative interactions, another category of safety developed, which is part of the hierarchy of needs (second and third segments of the pyramid). The school did not make him feel safe and did not establish a feeling of being wanted or that he belonged. If a negative situation occurred, the solution for the school was simple: "You would kick me out." The gang life had a stronger impact on developing that foundation, unfortunately in a negative manner, and enhanced the versus and axial codes. To further understand P1's educational experience, I asked him if he was ever told *why* he had to study math and other subjects.

Tom. Did they ever tell you why it was important to study math or history?

P1. Naw, I never had any of that. No, and I suck at math. No. I couldn't tell you now. Naw…nobody told…I could remember. Naw, what I'm saying? I couldn't even tell you my math teacher. That's how bad it is. They just said do this and never why or how we are going to use math.

The message is that there was no explanation or meaning as to why they had to study math. It is unfortunate that P1 cannot even remember the teachers name but can remember that he told the students to do it his way. The lack of proper instruction could be that reason for the lack of motivation for continuous learning. The following response was interesting in that he had a favorable reaction to another teacher because she took the time to make P1 feel special. The implication was that the conversational style was transactional instead of linear.

P1. I could only tell you about one teacher, and that's Ms. Petree…because I had a crush on her. And I think I was like in third grade. Ms. Petree, that's the only name of a teacher I can remember. She somewhat made me feel special.

Another teacher reaction to P1's behavior was that the teacher just "popped" him, and that became a feeling of hatred. The two different approaches that had opposite effects on P1's behavior. One was positive through an interaction of making him feel special, and the other had the opposite effect. His attitudes changed from one of respect to one of hatred. The teacher's approaches are two different motivational techniques that lead to two different outcomes. One is transactional, and the other is linear—a more negative approach to communication.

> **P1.** And Mr. Samson (*pseudonym*), Mr. Samson was the Black guy that popped me. You know, and boy, I hated him. But anyways, I mean it all depends on the school you are around…the school you are going to. I just think it's the environment in the schools play a part in the choices that we decided to take.

P1's comments indicate the role of the environment, which includes attitudes and norms. The attitude of the teachers and administrators have a tremendous impact on the behavior of the students, which could cause further resentment, apathy, anger, or could have a positive return, if presented properly. P1's attitude toward his math teacher was an emotional category of hatred based on the axial code of negative interactions. P1's next statement reflects his attitude and values toward his criminal activity and that his was responsible, not the school. He also mentioned that the school did not help him change his mindset but, by the school's action, further enhanced his criminal activity.

> **P1.** Because that school did not put a gun to my head and tell me to go sell drugs, go be in a gang, or go to jail. It's not the school's fault. But the area the school just happens to be in, happens to carry all these kinds of people here, and when you have all these same-minded people, you have violence, you have whatnot.

In the following section, P1 mentioned that denial by both prison officials and school administrations is an indicator for conditions in the facilities. P1's attitude is that both organizations try to avoid the subject by not truly addressing the issues. This is an indicator of the environment and apparent values of the organizations.

> **P1.** You can't go to a prison and say none of these guys are gang members, that's not going to work. So you can't go to that school and say none of you guys are D, E, F students. You are all straight As.

The response indicates a thought process to the mindset of the individuals, including gang members, students, teachers, and administrators who establish the policies based on the environment. In the next series of questions, the emphasis was on P1's perception of how the schools could improve the situation. His attitude was that the school really did not care and inferred that they did not know how to handle the situation. By P1's answer, he is implying that he wished they did care and show empathy toward the students, so he could change his lifestyle and become a better person.

> **Tom.** What can schools do to improve situations?
> **P1.** What schools can do to improve situations is give a damn about us. Give a damn about their teacher, give a damn about their job, about what they want to prove or whatnot, regardless of the skin color. Regardless of the skin color or whatever, you are there as a teacher, you are there to teach me, to teach him—the White kid, the Black kid, and this and that and that. That's what you are there for.

P1 also mentions that students are not motivated to get an education or told what subjects' matter, how they are taught, and why they are important. The perception of apathy prevails, and the best way to improve the educational system is for the teachers to do their jobs that they were hired for. This comment can be interpreted to mean that there has to be more professional development in the areas of transactional communication, understanding cultural differences, motivating students to want to learn, and answering the question of *why* education is important. The implication is that the process has to clarified, not only for the teachers but also the students. P1 further explains his perception of teachers' attitudes toward difficult students.

> **P1**. We are there for different reasons. And try to get the attention of the guy or the girl. Don't just—this kid's not going to listen, I don't want him in my class anymore. And it's in your brain that, okay, I'm not going to waste my time with this kid.
>
> **Tom**. Yeah, you are already branded.
>
> **P1**. Why? Why am I going to waste my time with this kid when I got this girl and this other guy over here who are just raising their hand question after question, wanting to learn, wanting to do this, wanting to do that? They are going to automatically go after them because they see something in them.

This reaction could also be a reflection on the lack of practical, purposeful, and value-driven education for all students, not only for the ones who want to learn but including the students who do not understand the true importance of education. This comment also increases the importance of the versus category by including other students against one another, not just the school against the students, thus creating a negative attitude toward all aspects in the school environment. I further wanted to explore if teachers aided the students who needed help.

> **Tom**. Did they offer to help in English or math or history?
>
> **P1**. Naw, you know what they...I don't see...I can't remember...I don't see how...I don't see why they would tell me or this. If they don't care, why waste their time with you? If I have an image of skipping class or sagging, flirting with the girls at school, okay, that don't have anything to do with your job to teach me, regardless of who I am or what I'm doing. You want to hurry up and report me to the teacher? You want to hurry up and report me to the principal? That's all you want to do. Report me real quick. You know...take the time to talk to me. Why don't you bring me outside and be like and say, "P1, P,1 why don't you leave that little girl alone? You know, how do you know if she like you, flirting with you? Leave her alone. Go flirt with somebody else," or somewhere else or something. Just explain...they don't take the time to do that.

P1 emphasizes the importance of being stereotyped by one's actions, whether it be by verbal actions or nonverbal reactions to the way one dresses. This stereotyping of students further leads to an us-versus-them mentality and a process of just "report to the principal." P1's statements also were a plea for help by stating, "They don't take the time to help." I further wanted to explore the reasons teachers gave as to the importance of taking certain classes like history, math, and English.

P1. Nay…they never told why history or math or English was important… they just told us to learn it so we could get a job. In history, they told us to memorize the dates and what happened. It was really boring. I hated math, especially algebra, because I could not…how I could use it. The teachers gave us the formulas and told us to memorize. Memorize what? Hey, Mr. Tom, it was not until you told us that history repeats itself and we do not want to make the same mistakes. You used the gang life as an example of how gangs were formed and how they are now an important part of life—for good or bad. You told me that math and algebra would help me in forming my own business by telling me that if I didn't know math, people would take advantage of me. It was you, Mr. Tom, that told me that I was the message, and people who didn't know me would be prejudice for or against me. Even in the way I passes out fliers for my new company. If I had poor messages, misspellings, etc., people would think that I would do a poor job.

This segment was recorded after the initial interview and included in this section to offer a progression of the thought process. The inclusion was to further clarify the importance of understanding the why of learning certain subjects. The significance of P1's comments offer clarification as to the importance of making these subjects relevant to meet the needs of the students. Using analogies that students can relate to through their own experiences can assist in answering the question of why these subjects are important. Teachers and administrators must develop an appreciation of the importance of *listening* to the students so the teachers can meet the needs of the individuals who really want to be helped and do not even know it. To fully understand the impact of seeking help from teachers, I was curious as to the reaction of other students.

TOM. If you went to a teacher and asked for help, what would the other people say about you?

P1. He brings it on himself. So, but you know it's just like I said, it's just the environment you are in. Some people…and you know pride plays a lot of part too, the image. Pride and image plays a lot. You don't want your homeboys thinking you are a punk. Or a punk or a pussy or a sissy or a nerd. Or this or that. Fuck this, fuck that. I ain't doing that shit. Man, I ain't sitting on that desk like that. Lean that shit to the side, you know. It's just image and pride. You want to be the tough guy for the prettiest girl there. Or you want to whoop the football star to try to take his girl. Just anything. You know, it's all image, and who knows more about the streets and just…

The importance for Rick and for many other students is the focus on image and pride, which develops the attitude of resentment, apathy, and one's identity. For P1, he had an image to uphold, and he felt it was important for others to view him in rebellious tough-guy manner. He also wanted the teachers to know who he was and that his attitude had a direct bearing on his negative desire to learn. This negative value enhanced his image as more important to his peers, even though it caused him problems in school. His pride not to be different than his associates caused him not to seek help, even though he wanted assistance. He felt that his groupthink mentality prevented him from initiating change in his approach to education and getting out of a negative environment.

Том. Tell me more.

P1. Sucker ass dude. Sucker ass dude. You going to college, bitch-ass dude? You going to high school, bitch-ass dude? You ask me, I'll answer for you…

The pressure from his peers and the fear of not acceptance caused P1 not to change his thought process or values. The school, according to P1, did not help or offer guidance as to how to break out of this mentality, and the school's lack of actions only further enhanced his negative reactions. The pressure to conform to the hostile environment was overwhelming, and his pride forced him to retain his image. With all these problems facing the students, whether they be the family structure, community organization, gang influence, or the school environment, I was curious as to P1's process by offering his solution to the problem.

Том. So what I'm seeing here is an endless cycle. It's a cycle we've got to break, and we got to figure out how to do it. What do you say is the answer or solution to the problem?

P1. It all comes down to…it all comes down to parents and teachers because growing up, that's who you see the most. Parents and teachers. You know… and explain. Hey look, this is this, and this is this. This is the way this is. These are the way things are. Like me, for example, my kids. My daughter hits fourteen, fifteen—other guys won't do what I'll probably do. And I'll sit down and talk to my daughter and say, "Look, you are fourteen, fifteen years old. You're a pretty girl, and I'm pretty sure these little boys are looking at your nice body, but you're going to have to be smart. They don't love you." I'll tell my daughter the game. And I'll let her know, look, this is the way it is. This is the way it is. I'm your dad, and I'd rather me tell you than another guy. Whatever, I'm gonna let you know how it is.

P1 suggests that parents and teachers have the potential to have the greatest impact on the lives the students. The fact that they spend so much time with the children is critical to the child's development. He also suggests that there must be communication among all concerned with boundaries and values established to offer guidance as to make the right decisions. P1 felt that it was his responsibility to talk to his daughter about the motives of some of the male students but indicated that the school could also support his value concept of morality. I wanted to pursue this topic, especially with his daughter's experiences in school.

Том. All right, with your daughter in school…fourteen, probably freshman or eighth grade or something like that—what's her school experiences like? What has she told you about her experiences?

P1. Which one?

Том. The fourteen-year-old.

P1. I don't have no kids. I'm saying if I had.

Tom. Oh, if you had…

I was surprised with his answer and that he did not have any children. He was using an analogy to emphasize a point of developing communication with children not only with parents but also for teachers to give guidance by explaining the effects of one's actions. He mentioned that there are people out there who have alternative motives and that one must be conscious of values in making decisions. P1 gave an example by using the experiences of a girl that he is dating.

> **P1.** But look, now if you want to go into that, look at this, this is what I tell you. This girl I'm dating, she has a daughter. She's fifteen. Very smart girl. As all the way to the top. All the way, and I told her about boys and their motives. My girlfriend, she's paying $30,000 grand a year for that school. And it's a small faith…it's a smaller Christian school, but she is paying $30,000 grand. And they got high people coming out of there. Because they don't have people sagging in there. They don't have people cursing. They don't have this, they don't have that. She's a real good girl. She had to get her daughter out of the public schools and get her into a place where she can survive.

The educational experience of the faith-based school is a completely different environment and is a versus code between public schools and faith-based institutions. In the public schools, especially inner city, the mindset is survival, whereas in the faith-based school, the attitude is for a purpose and value-driven educational experience. I felt it was important to contact P1's girlfriend have a conversation about her perceptions. The conversation was conducted in September of 2018 and lasted for forty-seven minutes. The girl P1 is dating felt that she had to get her daughter out of the public schools due to the lack of students being challenged and into a private school environment, where there was a strong focus on values and the importance of an education.

The decision to transfer her daughter to a private school was also based on the school's ability to cater to the needs of the individual student. She teaches in Department of Children's Service (DCS) facility and is aware of the difficulties that teachers in the public school sector have to go through. Problems ranging from micromanagement to curriculum design and the lack of support from the administrators that demand statistics to verify performance. Another difficulty she faced was that she was told to use the "common core" agenda in teaching math, and that logic she had difficulty comprehending. She was also frustrated with teaching to the test mentality and not using formative testing as a learning tool.

I related her comments to the lack of developing Professional Learning Communities (PLC), as described by Richard DuFour, Rebecca DuFour, Robert Eaker, and Thomas Many in their book *Learning by Doing* (2010). Her students are the ones that the public schools have neglected or could not handle and passed on to other agencies. She also mentioned that the problems her students have come from a conglomerate of factors ranging from dysfunctional families and communities to cognitive behavior disorders. The conversation that I had with P1's girlfriend was extremely fascinating in that there are so many similarities between her DCS school, the public school system, and the educational programs in the jails and prisons. Her perception is that the problems with the incarcerated individual started not only with the family and communities but also with the public school educational system. Another paper has to be written about the teacher's perception of public schools in relation to their students' criminal activities.

I continued with P1's interview to further explore the differences in public education and the private sector environment.

> **Tom.** So it's a different environment.
> **P1.** It's a different environment. Her dad has plenty of money. So that school…you go to that school, you can go from kindergarten all the way to twelfth grade.

Now some of those people actually go to Rhodes in Memphis that Rhodes College that's expensive…and she's pretty bright, and she wants to be a doctor.

By talking to P1's girlfriend and by his own experiences, the perception—the process of settings goals, having a dream, and being challenged to fulfill those desires—is the basic difference between the public school and faith-based experiences. P1's goal is to stay out of prison and his girlfriend's daughter is to become a doctor. The conversation also reenforces the categories of goal settings and having a dream of accomplishment. It also adds another category of having a positive educational path to achieve their goals. I asked P1 if he thought parents and teachers could get together and come up with strategies to collaboratively change the system.

> **P1.** Yeah, I mean, that was even based on the movie *Lean on Me*…you know, when the principal tried to go talk to the parent. "Your daughter is pregnant." Whatever. "I don't care what she is." I mean, you can only do so much. I mean…but yes, I think with the parents and the teachers, I think a lot of these people, you know…I think a lot would be changed. Cell phones got to get out of there.
>
> **Tom.** I tend to agree there.
>
> **P1.** No, I'm going to tell you that now—cell phones got to get out. Cell phones are going to keep stuff…cell phones just have to be banned from school, man. I don't know why…I mean, that's why I say it's hard with the world we grow up in now.

P1's perception is that due to technology, we are living in a fast-paced society with instant access to all aspects of communication. He relates instant communication to what "the mind sees, the mind thinks" and how times have changed due to what is conceived to be normal. Parents and teachers have to take control of the cell phone situation and develop a process to leave the phones in backpacks or not in school at all, according to P1. The collaboration between parents and teachers could help change the mindset of all concerned individuals by showing the students that the parents and the school officials are in charge.

> **P1.** When we were growing up. who the hell is going to dare to come shoot the damn school up? We dare you to come up with that shit, we'll beat the dogshit out of you. Now, it's normal. Hey, you know another kid got…where at this time? New York. Oh, shit yeah, no telling, the next time it's probably going to be San Diego. It's sad, but it's normal. Now if you want to talk about the streetwise, gangwise, or gangster mentality from whatever by the school, school doesn't teach you how to be a gangster. You know or this or that. What teaches you to try and be that person is by what you see. What the eye sees, the mind thinks. You know, you don't think about something and then see it. No. I see that, and I go, "Oh, okay, well, that's this, and that's' that." What the eye sees, the mind thinks.

The influence of technology is another category to be added to the problems facing the students in our society and how values are redefined by the use of technology and by "what the mind sees." P1's conversation goes on to further explain the feelings or lack of caring that really is the main cause of dysfunctional behavior. He relates his personal feelings to a movie, *A Bronx Tale*, that in the end, nobody really cares.

> **P1.** When the eye sees gold, like the movie *A Bronx Tale*, the little kid growing up. The little kid growing up. You know, Mafia dude, Mafia dude. His dad. Hey, stay away from that shit, man. Ah no, you are a sucker, man, you are a sucker. We want to be playing out there with all the people and whatnot… whatnot. And I can relate to that because at the end when he's at Sonny's funeral, he's looking at the guy like, you're right, nobody cares. Everybody's drinking, everybody's chilling, and he told him so. Man, they all acted like nobody just died. So he's like, nobody really cares. So you got to realize…it's sad that it took death for him to realize…that, hey man, this ain't what's up. Nobody cares. Is this the way everybody is going to act when I die?

The theme that is also being developed is the importance of empathy and that someone cares about the individual. P1 further explains that while he was incarcerated, the most important message he received was a simple birthday or Christmas card. P1's, conscious or subconscious, message was that maybe a caring thought from someone could have changed his behavior and that emotional support is critical; and without that support, pain of loneliness is the outcome.

> **P1.** In the movie *A Bronx Tale*? It's just like me…I went to prison in 2002— '02, '03, '04, '05. I went back '06 and got out in '07. I got out late '07, went back July '09, and just got out again 2016. And this time—naw, hell naw. Nobody cares. Nobody cares. Nobody was there for me. That's what changed me. You know what, at the end of the day, what mattered to me most was birthday cards, Christmas cards. If you don't have that emotional support from out there, you ain't going to make it.

P1 offers solutions to the problem, and it is based on the principle of listening and not judging us. He emphasizes the importance of getting everyone involved, especially government officials who will influence their constituents to initiate change. The problem P1 perceives is that too many people know the answers without consulting the people who are in trouble and need help. The perception is that nobody really cares, especially about the inner-city low-income school district because the people there have already been prejudged as individuals who cannot control their own lives.

> **P1.** But who will take the time to go to these low-income schools? It's not us. It's having the people, man, to look at us a certain way. You know, don't look at me like…oh, he's a sagger. There's not a lot of people out there like you, Mr. Tom. There is, but the thing is one in New York, one in New Jersey, one is over here, one is over here, one is in the middle, one's over here, and they are all trying to climb, but just the world is too big. We have to come together. Now just think about all these—uh-oh, here comes, Tom, now here comes this one…Oh, hey, Senator So-and-So, hey, how are you doing?" "Oh, I'm over here following these guys over here. They've got an educational pro-

gram on for kids and gang members." Just whatever, just trying to—oh, just help me, Mr. Senator. Once you've got him, everyone else comes flocking into place. The best thing you can do, man, is just explain. Just try to explain, you know, and agree with them. If I go to school and think I know it all. Then…naw, Tom, that ain't how you do it…Mr. Tom, naw, you're lying, you're lying. Well, what you need everybody to do is to listen to us and not think that you are better and that we cannot help.

The concept that P1 is trying to explain is that there are solutions, but all people have to be heard. P1 suggests that the powers in control must take the time and go into the inner-city schools and talk to the people involved and get their input. Not just go in and make a pseudo-appearance but actually listen the needs. He also implies that there is a different need between inner-city schools and suburban districts, and the needs have to be addressed differently. State standards apply to all districts, and maybe that approach is clarifying the academic achievement gap between districts. In reading into what P1 is inferring, the mindset of all factions of society have to be involved to develop a process of correcting this dilemma. The resolution must come from the people directly involved, or they will not take ownership in the final decision.

TOM. So you got to force the issue and force the people to come together.

P1. On where? The schools…the gangs…the senators, my parents, businesses.

TOM. For the school, whether it be senators—

P1, *interrupts.* You've got to be heard. That's the only way. You've got to be heard, Mr. Tom. You've got to be heard. You have to be heard. That's the only way it's going to be done. Because there is more against you than with you. They need the truth and a leader who will give them the truth and tell them what to do. And this right here, whatever you are trying to do for betterment, it's not just for inmates, it's for everybody.

TOM. I think…I think what you just said is that you summed up the entire thing. We all have to come together, and we have to come together.

P1. We just need one person in power of it all, and you need that one and just keep going where they can be heard. But as long as you're alone…with all due respect, it's not going to…you need…you need…you need to be heard on that. You need to be heard on that. And for example, a lot of people ain't with it. Some centers are like, lock 'em up, throw away the key.

TOM. Yeah, this is where we have to change the mindset of society to demand more practical and purpose-driven education with values. Because if we don't, nothing's going to change.

P1 is inferring that all factions of society have to come together and develop a process of ownership in the decisions made to enhance not only the schools but the family and community. One of Rick's examples of coming together is to establish guidelines for the usage of the internet and gang video games and explain how this technology is actually preventing individuals from getting an accurate picture of reality, thus creating negative values. "If you got your kid growing up playing *Grand Theft Auto* all damn day and he thinks it's fun, he's actually going to want to see this shit in real life."

P1. And I've heard there's…let me give you an example. Those two little girls I think in Pennsylvania about two years ago. They killed their little friend behind that face mask. They took her out to a gravel road and killed her, stabbed her to death like fifty, sixty times. That's what I'm saying. What causes that? Could it be the internet or video games? Our gang members don't do that. We would spank that little girl for even thinking of doing some stuff like that. You know, we hurt each other, and that's what congressmen, you, or everybody here needs to feel safe about. We hurt each other.

The message that P1 was trying to convey was that society has to be careful in what is acceptable and what is not. Also, that even with gangs there are boundaries that cannot be crossed, or there are consequences for one's actions, thus reinforcing that even gangs have values. Rick further went on to explain conditions in prison that were similar to the conditions in the public school system.

P1, I can only tell you about…prison sucks too. Prison doesn't make…they want to jack you for everything, they want to jack you for your shower. No, Rick, not even going to worry about that, no shower. They are going to come into your cell and take all your shit. No, you know that's not right. That breeds anger and hatred. So when we are released, we are released with all this anger and hatred that was built up. It was the same way in school: we left with a hatred for the teachers, for other students, and in most cases, a hatred of ourselves.

Tom. I think that's a good way to end this conversation, but what I do want to do is say thank you. And I would say it is my position that I don't care about your past. I care about your future.

P1. Yeah, but—

Tom. And this is one of the things that we have to work on. Say, hey, forget about the past, but we are going to work for the future. And it's getting there. If we don't, we are not going to change the system.

P1. I can't do nothing. I can't do nothing if they are going to keep holding onto my past. I ain't nobody no more. Let me vote, let me vote, let me have my rights to carry my firearm. I've already paid my dues. Y'all are still holding this against me. I can't live like this. It's not letting me move on with my life. The state government always wants to go back. Well, you should give us a chance. If I go somewhere and try to ask for a job, oh no, we are this and that. Okay, Mr. Tom went in, and they say, "Mr. Tom, what's going on? Oh, Professor Tom, how are you doing today? I need a real big favor today. One of my guys needs a job." "Okay, sure." Oh…him. I just told him we aren't hiring." You know, but that's what I'm saying, it's not…it's who you know.

Tom. It's not an easy job, but we are making inroads. We are going to make a difference, and you are going to make a difference.

P1: I just want to work, pay my bills, and I don't want to go back to prison.

There is a lot of frustration not only for the system but for himself. P1 realizes that he made many mistakes and that his punishment was for his actions. Throughout the interview, several themes started to develop, and the main one was the cry for help that was not recognized by the authorities. He felt he had to establish an image that was consistence with his peers. His pride caused him not to seek help, and for that, he suffered. In P1's perception, the school was not there for him; and for that reason, he got into trouble. The next interview was with a female who liked school but felt the system did not assist her when she needed help.

Interview II

The next interview was conducted at 7:00 a.m. on a rainy day in September of 2018 at the DCSO jail facility in Nashville, Tennessee, and lasted just over eighteen minutes before she was recalled back to her cell. The person selected was an individual who liked school and was a good student until family conditions caused anger behavior problems that affected her socially and her attitude toward school. She was suspended from school and eventually dropped out school in the tenth grade. P2 is a twenty-four-year inmate who was convicted of prostitution, armed robbery, and assault, and was waiting to be sentenced. She attended the practical, purposeful, and value-driven HiSET class until she got transferred to another facility. Her test scores in math, reading, and comprehension were sufficient to pass the HiSET test. With her ability, I had her tutor other inmates in those areas, and she was well respected for her ability to relate the subject matter in terms that could be understood by the other inmates.

In conversations with P2 in class, I found out that she is a very talented individual who lost all motivation to learn. She was court-ordered to take this class, and fortunately she began to change her attitude. Her desire was to become an outcast from the social norms, and she did so by becoming an aggressive and angry individual. Tattoos became her identity as a sign of resentment because no one cared, so why should she? That was her perception of reality and became a process code for her behavior problems.

> **Tom.** Welcome and thank you for participating in this voluntary interview. The questions I ask will pertain to why you are here and not what you did or how you did it.
>
> **P2.** I feel like it was my anger, and I felt like I was always being pushed. I was just being pushed.
>
> **Tom.** Tell me more about why you were angry. (*Pause*) Was it your family environment?
>
> **P2.** *No.* My parents split up when I was thirteen and could not find my dad, and my mom never knew how to show love.

P2 had a two-parent structure that was perceived by her to be normal. She was involved in extracurricular activities, did well in school, and developed friends in her neighborhood. She was expected to have good grades and to excel in athletics. The axial code of interactions developed a theme of support and acceptance by her classmates. The problems started when her parents separated, and she lost contact with her father. She told me in class that she never knew why her parents separated and that the absence of her father was extremely painful. She blamed the separation on herself, and her logic was that her father would have contacted her if it wasn't her fault.

The theme that enhanced the emotional code was of anger and possible miscommunication of not understanding the reason for the separation and lack of contact from her father. Her mother's focus was on the necessity of supporting the family and unfortunately not communicating with her children. "My mother never knew how to show love." This emotional code also further enhanced Maslow's third stage of the importance of belonging and love. The themes that began to develop were the importance of the family structure, the lack of showing love, and demanding higher expectations and results. The foundation of the hierarchy of needs was there. The parents gave the children a home, food, clothing, etc. and even made them feel safe. But the pyramid started to collapse when the parents separated and the father left without further contact. The next category that was added was additional trauma that eventually caused her behavioral problems.

> TOM. I understand that parental separation and the perceived lack of love could cause your anger issues, but what else was there to influence you in your decisions? Peer groups, gangs, other relatives…
>
> P2. No gangs, I was by myself. I was okay even with the separation, but when my niece died when I was thirteen, things started to compound. I was good in school, but when my niece passed away, things started to fall apart.
>
> TOM. Tell me more, what else happened?
>
> P2. My mom moved us to Jacksonville, Florida. I liked were I was and did not want to move.

The environment changed, and P2 had trouble adapting. She lost contact with her father, mother was too busy supporting the family, niece died, and they moved to another community. Besides adding trauma as a category, adapting to change must be considered as an important factor in her behavior patterns by enhancing the process code. In her hometown, she had a peer group of acceptance and enjoyed participating in school activities. Her identity was that she was an intelligent student, a good athlete, and had good friends. The problems started to escalate when they moved, and she felt she received no support from the new school or classmates.

> TOM. What was it like moving to a new school?
>
> P2. It was awful. I hated it, and I hated the other students. I hated my mother for making us move, and I hated my sister for joining the Army and moving to Maryland. I hated myself because everything was happening to me. Why me? I asked.
>
> TOM. What type of support did you get from your new school?
>
> P2. None…no…they just told us what we had to do and do it. No type of help or program.

The perception by P2 was that there was no help because they really didn't care about her. The codes of axial, emotion, and process developed categories of relationships, anger, hatred, and linear instruction. I asked her about her classmates and if they helped her assimilate into this new environment. Her answer was interesting in that she began to take responsibility for her actions.

> P2. Students I don't think I gave them a chance to like me. It was my attitude. My niece passed, my dad not being around, my sister gone, my mother always working. I just got angry, and I felt there was no support, and…I didn't seek it either. They did not offer either. Why would they…

P2's answers further enhanced the primary codes by stating the process that she went through that caused her behavior problems. The categories of anger and the lack of support became a segment of emotional codes. New categories were established through her responses and that was of individual responsibility and the acceptance of other people's reaction to her. I continued with the support question, and I asked about her teachers and if they ever volunteered to help her.

> **P2.** No. At first, they were nice, but that soon changed. I didn't get alone with other students, didn't try in class…I was labeled as a troublemaker. I think I just it was just me, and I was angry why we moved, and I was mad…I got into fights, yelled a lot, and I dropped out of school in the tenth grade.
>
> **Tom.** Where did you go, and what did your mother say?
>
> **P2.** I just ran away and haven't talked to her. I hit the streets…tried to find my sister in Maryland. I survived any way I could. Selling drugs, stealing…

P2 eventually made it the Nashville area and continued her criminal behavior. She was arrested several times and is facing jail sentences not only in Davidson County but in surrounding communities in Tennessee. The code of process identifies her behavior pattern and explains the category of recidivism through the category of survival. I wanted to pursue this conversation, but she was called back to her unit. Unfortunately, she was transferred to another facility before I could meet with the following week. In a previous conversation with P2, I asked her and the class questions about purpose, goals, and dreams. Most of the members never had a purpose except to survive. They never dreamed or set goals, they had nightmares, but P2 dreamed of doing something positive. P2 wanted to get certified as a hairstylist and eventually have her own business. The reason for this change in attitude was to "make people look good so they could feel better about themselves." Her statements reenforced the codes by accepting that there was a process of continuing education, the importance of axial relationships or interactions in helping develop a new thought process, and the emotion of making people feel better about themselves. The category of setting goals became a formative approach to change one's lifestyle.

I am going to miss talking to P2 because I feel she has so much to offer. I feel she was an individual who fell through the cracks in the system, and maybe the eventual outcome could have been totally different if someone offered support or just listened to her. In one of my last questions to P2, I asked her how she is going to make it. Her reply was, "I no longer have to do it myself."

The information from the equity audits and the responses from the questionnaire, focus group, and one-on-one interviews offered clarification to the research question but also developed further curiosity for further discussions from the incarcerated women. The topics ranged from White privilege, White guilt, biases in education, and solutions to the problems facing the incarcerated individual and solutions for general improvement of the educational system.

Group Discussion

The discussion was held in the program room of the annex at the jail facility in October of 2018. I did not have permission to record the conversation, so I am using my notes and notes from my associate teacher, Tiffany Manning, to record the answers to the questions. The topic was White privilege, and that conversation led to White guilt, prejudice, and bias in educational instruction. I purposely tried not to lead the conversation with my biases by asking direct questions, and I did ask follow-up questions and clarifications by using examples or analogies for their responses. The class initially started with of seven of my students, and three more joined in after they were cleared to leave their cells. There were five Caucasians, two Hispanics, and three African Americans. The session started at 7:25 a.m. and finished at 8:03 a.m. The names of the participants are not included for security and confidentiality concerns and replaced with P1, P2, etc. The ethnic background of the participants is indicated within a parenthesis: Caucasian (W), African American (B), Hispanic (H).

> **TOM (W).** What does the phrase "White privilege" mean?
>
> **P1 (B).** It means that when a White person is pulled over by a cop, they don't get a ticket.
>
> **TOM.** Okay…tell me more. Have you ever been pulled over and given a ticket by a White or Black cop?
>
> **P2 (B).** All the time.
>
> **TOM.** Did you deserve to get a ticket?
>
> **P1(B).** Um…yes. I was speeding, but I was running late, and they did not give me a break.
>
> **TOM.** Have you ever been given a warning from a Black cop?
>
> **P2 (B).** No…they wouldn't give me a break either.
>
> **TOM.** I got pulled over by a White state trooper for speeding, and he let me go.
>
> **P1 (B).** See. You got White privilege.
>
> **TOM.** I guess I did. I was speeding on I-24, and when I saw the state trooper turn around and come after me, I pulled over and waited. When he got to car, I rolled down my window, and before he could say a word, I thanked him for stopping me. I told him I was daydreaming and wasn't paying attention to the speed. He told me that this was the first time in twenty years that anyone has ever thanked him for stopping them. He gave me a warning ticket. My question is, was this because of my race or my attitude?
>
> **P3 (W).** Hey, I am going to try that the next time I am stopped. I guess it was maybe both, but I think it was because of your attitude toward the police.
>
> **P2 (B).** But, Mr. Tom, you don't understand. You are pulled over when you do something wrong. I am pulled over because the cops assume I did something wrong, and I get scared that they will search my car or question me about something that went down in the neighborhood that I didn't have anything to do with.
>
> **TOM.** I know. It is wrong, but what are we going to do about it, or what are you going to do about it?

This was an interesting exchange that represented a versus coding of race and attitude toward specific situations of being pulled over by the police. The axial code was fascinating in that the relationship between Black policemen and the Black students were similar to the interactions with White policemen. I wanted to further discuss White privilege in the context of community and education.

> **TOM.** I admit there was and probably still is White privilege, but has it changed over the years, especially in the communities?

P4 (W). There was a time when Blacks could only ride in the back of a bus or drink out of a certain water fountain. I was told that there were White-only public swimming pools, and when the law was passed that allowed Blacks to swim there, one pool was filled with dirt. I think that was in Nashville by Centennial Park.

Tom. I remember seeing a sign on a side door to a movie theater in Kentucky that read "Blacks Only." How has the situation changed?

P5 (B). It has changed and for the better. We can sit anywhere on a bus, go through the front door of a movie theater. But I still am conscious of where I am and have the feeling that people are watching me.

Tom. Why?

P5 (B). I don't know...it is just a feeling.

P1 (B). From talking to my grandparents, times have changes for the better, but it seems like we are more segregated today in the areas that we live than before. Maybe that is not reality, but just a feeling that I got.

Tom. Statistics show that in the Nashville area, there are neighborhoods of a certain racial makeup. Blacks live in the northern and western areas, whereas Hispanics live in the southeast section of Davidson County. I have not heard from any of my Hispanic friends.

P6 (H). We live in the Nolensville area with all of our relatives and friends. We feel safe there.

P7 (H). We are comfortable with our culture, food, friends, customs, and we speak the same language. People would come here from Mexico or other South American countries, and we would find commonality.

P8 (W). I grew up not far from Nolensville but attended an almost all-Black school. That is where I became street smart.

Tom. What do you mean street smart?

P8 (W). We all had to, just to survive. Some of my best friends are Black. There was a group of us that struggles to fit in anywhere. We were misfits and had to be tough. That is where I got into trouble, and that is where I had to learn that I had to fend for myself.

Tom. By attending a diverse school and living in a diverse community, did you feel you had White privilege?

P8 (W). Hell no. White privilege didn't keep me out here (jail).

The dynamics of community developed versus coding and a category of segregation. The process code of moving into a "like" community was prevalent with the Hispanics and hindered assimilation into other cultures. The main aspect that I wanted to discuss was if "White privilege" and "biases" were prevalent in the school system. The first session ended, and the discussion continued the following Friday from 7:15 a.m. to 8:10 a.m.

Tom. Welcome back, and as I mentioned last week, I want to continue the discussion on White privilege, biases, and White guilt. Thank you for your responses and your participation. Last week we talked about the general perceptions of White privilege and the influence it has on the community.

Today I want to expand that thought process and discuss this topic in regard to schooling.

P4 (W). I have thought about it throughout the week, and yes, there is White privilege, but the thought that goes through my mind is that I earned what I got, even going to jail. I don't like it, but I earned it. I got a good job because I was qualified for the job, not because of my race. I studied hard and got good grades—they were not given to me, I had to earn them. (She is one of the tutors that helps other students.)

P8 (W). I did not get any White privilege. I got sent to jail.

Tom. Okay, what are your thoughts on White privilege?

P2 (B). White privilege exists, especially in the suburbs. They get better schools, better neighborhoods, better teachers, better everything.

Tom. Okay, tell me why that occurs.

P2 (B). They don't have the crime that we do, and nobody wants to help us. Teachers come, and then they go, especially the good ones. The Whites get special treatment that we as Blacks don't get.

Tom. Okay, why do you think that?

P2 (B). I don't know. It seems they have it so easy compared to us.

Tom. What kind of community do they live in? Describe White suburbia.

P5 (B). They have nicer homes, cleaner neighborhoods, better schools.

Tom. What kind of family structure do you perceive exists in the suburban areas?

P5 (B). Probably similar to ours, except they have two parents for support and more money.

Tom. That is a big difference. What kind of ethnic makeup is there in White suburbia?

P1 (B). A lot of white families, but also Asians, people from India and Pakistan, and rich Blacks who have moved out of the hood.

Tom. Are you saying that White privilege encompasses more than just being "white" but also a crosscultural makeup of "earned privilege"?

P1 (B). No...yes, it is both, but why did I have to grow up here and not in a suburban community?

Tom. That I cannot answer, except say, what are you going to do about it?

The discussion continued to develop into an us-versus-them code with categories of "earned privilege" and "victimhood." The discussion continued on the reason of *why* there was such a big difference between the two environments. All the participants except for one individual grew up with a single parent as head of the household, and that parent figure was usually a mother or grandmother with no father figure to act as a role model. They all had children while they were in high school, except for one. This has been the trend with all the female participants: growing up in a single-parent environment, having children while in school, and no father figure. These situations develop categories of the importance of *support* and *role models*.

Tom. All of you have been in my classes for some time, and we have developed rapport or understanding that I care about your future and that by participating in these discussions, you will be helping others. With that being said,

I am going to ask you a personal question. Did having a baby while you were in school have any effect on your education?

P2 (B). Definitely. I had to take care of my baby, and I had to get help with babysitting. I could not concentrate on school.

P5 (B). My grandmother helped me, but it was hard. I liked going to school because I could get away and sleep. I was constantly tired.

P7 (H). My family helped me a lot, but I felt embarrassed at school when milk would leak from my breasts. Some of the students, even my friends, made fun of me.

Tom. What you are telling me is that having a baby made a big difference in your schooling. What about the suburban girls who got pregnant? How did they survive?

P1 (B). They had the money and family support.

Tom. How did they get the money?

P1 (B). From their parents.

Tom. Where did their parents get the money?

P1 (B). From their work. They had jobs, or they owned their own business.

Tom. Do you think their parents had an education?

P1 (B). Yes.

Tom. Now compare your situation to the suburban girl who got pregnant and had a baby.

P1 (B). I think I know where you are headed with these questions, and I think it goes back to choice in decisions that were made.

The process code further developed by stipulating that there is a course of action in determining one's future. Family support, education, and hard work develops opportunities for perceived success. The categories family support, importance of education, hard work, consequences for actions, and decision-making help develop a course of action to change the mindset from fixed to growth. The next series of questions were based on biases in education and if they had an influence on the quality of instruction.

Tom. Did you feel that some teachers or administrators had a bias toward you or your ethnic background?

P6 (H). I think the teachers did not understand us and thought of us as slow learners. The problem was that we did not understand the teachers.

P7 (H). Some teachers liked us, and others I thought wondered why we are here. Just because I am part Hispanic doesn't mean that I don't want to learn. Just give me a chance.

P8 (W). I think they did not like me because I was a troublemaker and had an attitude that I didn't care. But I did care, but I didn't know what to do or how to tell them that I did care.

P1 (B). Gangs made a difference in the attitude of the teachers and administrators in their biases. The gangs even had a bias toward some of the teachers. Especially the ones that they could work.

P3 (W). I think the teachers had a bias for kids who had a positive attitude and treated them differently than students with poor attitudes. I guess that is normal. I feel the same way.

Bias is an important factor in the individual's perception of how they are treated. The axial code of interactions was based on biases that the students perceived to be true and explained why the student failed. Biases became another category in the perception of the educational experience. The next question was based on "White guilt" and the perceived role it had on the students' mindset.

Tom. *White guilt* is the harm that White people did to minorities in the past and present, especially the Black community, that they feel ashamed or responsible for. Did you feel you were treated differently because of white teachers having a guilt complex about how their ancestors treated your ancestors?

P2 (B). Do you mean teachers giving me the benefit of the doubt because I am Black and just passing me on?

Tom. You tell me.

P2 (B). I think some of the teachers did not care, but others felt sorry for me. I mean I never heard of that excuse before. If they just passed me on because they felt sorry for me, they really did not do me any favors. They actually hurt me because I attended high school but could not read or understand basic math.

P3 (W). It think it is meaningless and has no bearing on our situation. I had no control over what white people or any other people did to others. Do I feel bad on what occurred? You bet I do, but I know I won't act that way.

P1 (B). If White guilt is feeling sorry for what their ancestors did to mine, then that is a greater form of racism. It is telling us we cannot make it by ourselves and that the Whites have to help us because they are superior. That is bullshit. Treat me like you would treat anyone else. I have been thinking a lot about this subject of White privilege over the past week, and I think it just doesn't matter anymore. It might have meant a lot to you, Mr. Tom, because of your age, but to us, it just doesn't matter. I feel I have the same opportunities as anyone else, and it is my decision on how react to those opportunities. I have made mistakes, and I have messed up, and I feel a lot of "guilt" for what I did. You don't have to take on the responsibility of being guilty for my actions. If you do, then you are making me a victim who has no responsibility for my own actions.

The session closed at 8:10 a.m. but could have and should have gone on for more discussion. The closing statement by P1 was a summation of the thought process, including attitudes, prejudices, and biases that influence the educational experiences. Her remarks indicated an attitude of individual responsibility and equality. As her teacher and as a researcher, I find her responses to be meaningful and from the heart. More importantly, they offer an opportunity for others to follow her example. P1 is being released from jail in the near future, and she plans on continuing her education. Even though the topic of White privilege was not the scope of this research, the discussion offered new insights into the thought process of the inmates and expand categories of not only educational influences but community, family, and individual responsibilities. The mapping of these codes and categories is chaotic but shows the complexity of the situation.

Mapping of Codes, Categories, and Themes

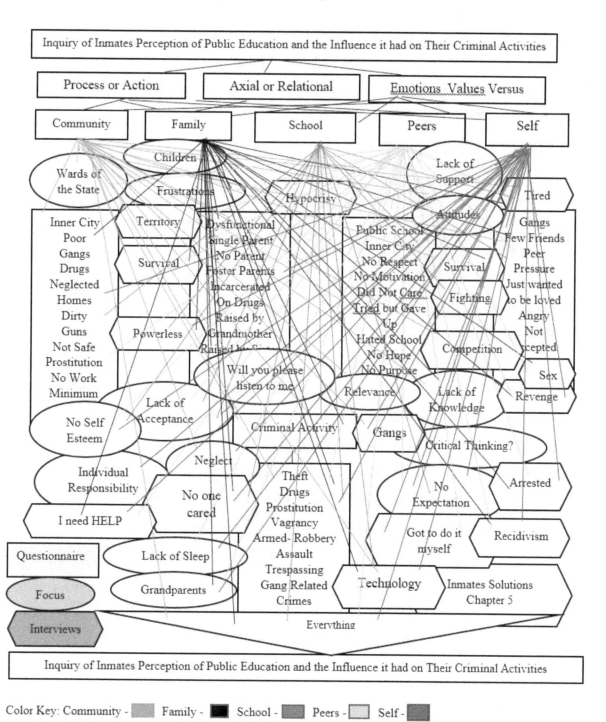

Figure 17. Chaotic Mapping

The chaotic mapping in figure 17 indicates the interaction of the categories and how not just one segment influences criminal behavior; but a combination of the community, family, schools, peers, and the self are the leading indicators.

Mapping of Codes, Categories, and Themes

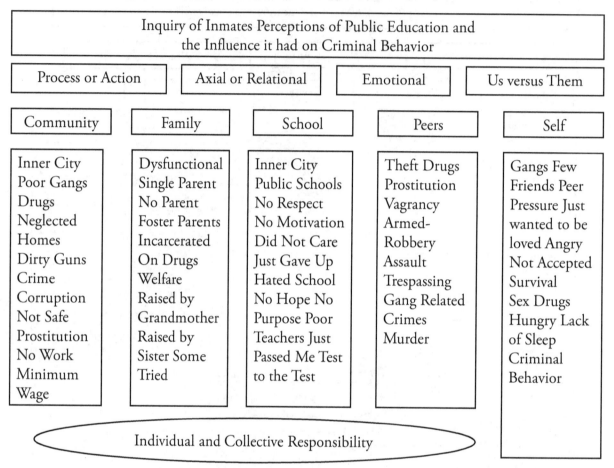

Figure 18. Clarification of Mapping and Coding for Themes and Theories

Figure 18 offers further clarification as to the difficulties facing the individual student, family, schools, peers, and community, but also that each segment interacts with the other. The theme that was developed by the students was that all segments have to come together to address the issues and come up with solutions.

Summary

The summary of this chapter was fascinating in that the participants individually and collectively shared experiences with their interactions with the public school system but also added categories of family, community, peers and self with numerous additional categories of explanations for their criminal behavior. The inquiry audit of the demographics helped develop an understanding as to the conditions or environment that the individuals endured. The academic achievement audit gave us an indication of the academic level of competence. The questionnaire was the foundation for further exploration of the initial research question and started to develop additional important subquestions to be considered to understand behavior patterns. The focus group clarified and offered support to the other participants by letting them know that they were not alone.

The interviews offered further perspectives to the influence of the family, community, peers, self, and education. The first interview with P1 was based on his negative experiences in school, and he offered demographic explanations that contributed to his criminal activity. P2 was much different in that she took responsibility for her actions but wished someone would have reached out to her to give her guidance or at least recognized the support and accepted it. Questions rose from lack of identity, peer pressure, dysfunctional families, and educational system not meeting the needs of the students. The mapping in figure 16 shows the chaos and connections between all aspects of society. The most important aspect of the process was the inclusion of secondary research questions and codes and categories that were not anticipated. Those additions had an influence on the development of various themes. I discuss the various theme implications of the findings and suggestions that the inmates have on improving the system in the next chapter.

CHAPTER 5

Implementations as Perceived by Inmates and the Researcher

The primary research question was an inquiry into inmates' perceptions of public school education and the influence it had on their criminal activity. After reading the questionnaire answers, conducting focus-group sessions, interviewing inmates, and offering a forum for discussion—the implications of their behavior became apparent. Survival, at any cost, became the motivating factor for their criminal activity. Their mental thought process was one of being in "social quicksand" with no hope to get out, especially with no help and the feeling that no one really cared. Several more subquestions developed, and the inmate-students offered explanations to the original research question and subquestions. But more importantly, the questions and answers developed themes and concepts to offer solutions to the research questions. The following table illustrates the potential themes that developed from the research questions.

Table 7. Themes

Research Questions	Themes
In what ways do inmates describe how their educational experiences influenced their criminal activity?	Negative Attitudes Peer pressure not to conform Lack of support from school officials Grade drop out of school Academic achievement gap Grade-level equivalency
What was the influence of the family?	Dysfunctional families caused criminal behavior. Single parent, grandparents, other relatives, including siblings.
What was the influence of the community?	Demographics of the community caused problems including broken-down conditions of neighborhood and no or few employment opportunities
What was the influence of peers?	Gang acceptance and the sense of belonging, student competition through image friends based on gang membership
What is the perception of yourself?	Victim of the environment Alone and forgotten Responsible for your own actions

Research Questions and Themes

These questions develop a foundation of knowledge for further research and, for this project, offers clarification as to the mindset of the individual by developing themes as to the reason *why*. The main concerns are the implications of the influence that society has on the incarcerated individuals. The mindset of being self-centered out of need to survive is detrimental. Not only to one's self but to the family, community, and the educational system. As I was conducting the research, Maslow's hierarchy of needs become a prominent explanation for behavior patterns that led to incarceration, not only in education but the family, community, peers, and self. Parallels are made to determine if the other categories and the themes have any influence in the family, community, peers, and self in determining a connection or relation to the hierarchy of needs. I began with the family and finished with the educational structure.

Family

Throughout the discussions and interviews, the family structure became a primary theme: a theme of dysfunction that led to the collapse of the pyramid of needs. Even though the inmates had in most cases the physiological needs of shelter, food, clothing, sleep, etc., the foundation was not a solid structure. Most of the inmates came from single-parent-family environment where the use of drugs was prevalent and caused financial hardship. Fast-food restaurants and school breakfast and lunch programs became the source for food. Twelve of the fourteen individuals of the focus group mentioned that their parents used drugs, and they had also been incarcerated. The safety level was also a concern to the students. Even though there was a sense of security at home, that security was often challenged by the female single parent who brought home different "boyfriends."

Often there was abuse and noise that caused a lack of sleep, causing the individual to go to school tired. The neighborhood also contributed to the lack of security. The next level is the need for belonging and the use of the word *love*. In the family structure for the inmate-students, this category was the most prevalent in their relationship with their parents, siblings, and extended family. Most of the students mentioned that they came from a dysfunctional family where there was only a single parent, and their only function was to be another number for welfare assistance. This mindset, true or not, is a major concern for the welfare of a child in a family environment.

One student mentioned that at the age of ten, she would visit her father in prison. She hated the experience of being frisked and going through all the security gates, but what she hated most was when she visited her dad, he always talked about himself and never once told her that he loved her. At the age of fourteen, a guy told her that he "loved her," and at the age of fifteen, she was pregnant, and he was gone. The pyramid collapsed, and she lost her self-esteem. The women mentioned they had little to no self-esteem and that they felt alone in their efforts to survive. Limited to no parental support, being unsure about their safety, and the perception of not belonging or being loved caused them to have self-doubt about their purpose. There were no goals or feelings of self-accomplishment, just surviving. The self-actualization never truly occurred, except in a negative manner. They truly believed that they lost all hope, that they were not going to get out of this family environment; and in actuality, they felt their family structure was a norm. I reminded them that 71 percent of their children will become incarcerated. The theme of a dysfunctional family structure became prevalent in determining attitudes and criminal behavior.

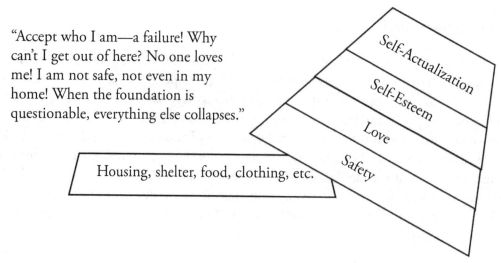

"Accept who I am—a failure! Why can't I get out of here? No one loves me! I am not safe, not even in my home! When the foundation is questionable, everything else collapses."

Figure 19. Hierarchy of Needs: Collapse of the Family

Community

The demographics of the community also was a detriment to fulfilling a positive self-actualization of accomplishment. The theme for the community became one of disrepair and the lack of an initiative to change or not knowing how to change. The pyramid of physiological needs was there, but under what conditions? The neighborhoods were run down and dirty; businesses were closing and leaving for a better environment. The jobs available were few and low-paying. Due to gangs, the neighborhoods were not safe. Gun fights, robbery, and armed assaults were common. According to one individual, churches were a common area to buy drugs. The only requirement was to become a member of a gang. Another theme developed, and that was with the communities' relation with politicians and the local police force. The perception was, "Politicians just wanted our votes. They promised everything and gave us nothing." The police were "crooked and belonged in jail," as stated by LaKeisha in a classroom conversation. The self-actualization was that the community was the norm, and there was no way out.

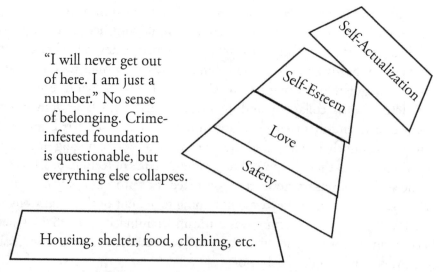

"I will never get out of here. I am just a number." No sense of belonging. Crime-infested foundation is questionable, but everything else collapses.

Figure 20. Hierarchy of Needs: Collapse of the Community

Peers

The theme for the relation to peers was one of establishing self-identify and developing an image based on the family and community expectations and acceptance. Unfortunately, there were few positive role models, and Maslow's hierarchy of needs became a standard and very influential in the recruitment for gangs. "You need a place to hang out, you need food, clothing. You can wear our colors, you need sex—no problem." The foundation of physiological needs was established and further enhanced by offering safety. "We will protect you. Anyone who bothers you, we'll take care of it." The third level of the pyramid is the social needs of the individual. The gangs offer friendship, the sense of belonging and that the group cares for you. "Hey, man…we love you, bro."

With the first three levels of the pyramid established, an individual has the feeling of being needed, that people care about them. The motivating force is now to gain respect and show the gang that their decision to be included was the right decision. But now one has to prove that the gang decision was correct. By accomplishing certain tasks, one can gain respect and even be promoted to a higher rank in the organization. By doing so, the mindset becomes, "Hey, I am important, and I can actually do the things that I was asked to do."

In the interview with Rick, he became a lieutenant because of his actions and gained the respect of the gang. By becoming a leader, his self-worth became a motivating factor in developing his self-esteem that he was important and that he could accomplish tasks when asked to do so. The self-actuation of the pyramid was critical for Rick in that he finally realized what he was doing was wrong, especially after a gang leader was chopped up and dumped into Galveston Bay. Rick retained his gang status while in prison for protection, but when released, he felt he had to escape the chains of this negative influence on his life and so something positive for his own survival and peace of mind. The social-acceptance aspect was vitally important to the research members: the sense of belonging became a motivating factor to join groups.

Unfortunately, there were few positive role models in the home, community, and among their peers. The lack of positive role models became another theme of importance in the behavior and attitude toward criminal activities. The positive role models became individuals who did not live in the area and had no direct relation with the students. Usually, rap artists were the ones that participants looked up to, but the reality was that they lived over there, and we lived here. The connections became the messages from the songs, either positive or negative. Those messages became an influence on who they wished they could be but, in reality, helped develop a false sense of identity.

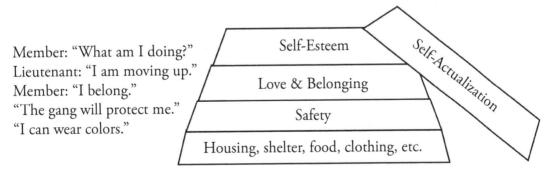

Figure 21. Hierarchy of Needs: Collapse of Peers and Gangs

Self

The self-portion of the pyramid of needs was extremely important to the women because it established a mindset of desires. Unfortunately, their desires became a theme of perceived reality, themes of failure, no goals, no dreams, no hopes, and no future. Their desire was to have a firm foundation of where they could live, free from harm, and a place where they felt they belonged and were loved. The mindset of desire was never accomplished, and therefore the reality became a sense of failure on their part. The self-actualization was that they felt they were not important enough or good enough to make a difference. Their focus became more self-centered just for survival.

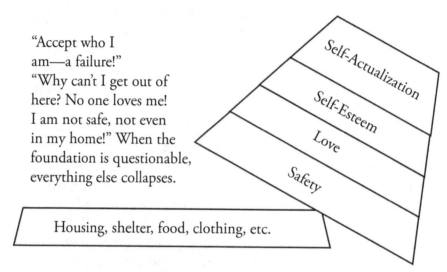

"Accept who I am—a failure!" "Why can't I get out of here? No one loves me! I am not safe, not even in my home!" When the foundation is questionable, everything else collapses.

Housing, shelter, food, clothing, etc.

Figure 22. Hierarchy of Needs: Perception of Self

Public Schools

The theme for the public school system became one of despair by being dictatorial, not understanding the needs of the students, being perceived with the sense of not caring. According to the research participants, the schools provided a structure, but most of the other physiological needs were negative. The schools provide food, water, and an academic format, but they also provided opportunities for sexual exploration, gang participation, and a mindset of negative attitudes toward authoritative figures. They did not like being told what to do, especially not know or understanding the *why* of the purpose. The schools in the inner city did not make them feel safe due to the negative actions of retaliation among their peers and school officials. With the first two segments of the pyramid, the participants did not feel they belonged and reacted through the use of anger and or retaliation by the use of physical force. Their self-esteem diminished when they failed assessments about subjects they did know or comprehended and really diminished when they were passed on to the next grade level without the basic knowledge or understanding of the subject matter. They felt like they were not important enough for the school system to offer more assistance to help them, and that became their self-actualization.

Another research question that immerged was if teachers and administrators received professional training in motivating students to achieve their greatest potential by emphasizing the importance of goals, values, and dreams. he perception of the women was that the teachers just taught the subject and never emphasized the practical application to meet their needs.

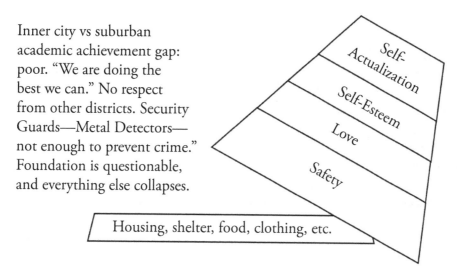

Inner city vs suburban academic achievement gap: poor. "We are doing the best we can." No respect from other districts. Security Guards—Metal Detectors—not enough to prevent crime." Foundation is questionable, and everything else collapses.

Self-Actualization
Self-Esteem
Love
Safety
Housing, shelter, food, clothing, etc.

Figure 23. Hierarchy of Needs: Perception of Public School Education

Maslow's hierarchy of needs was originally intended to be a positive model for achieving self-actualization of success as written by Maslow in 1943 (pp. 370–396). In this portion of the research, the hierarchy became a negative structure for failure and self-destruction.

Motivation and Mindset

The implication that the inmates are labeled and have no hope for success are difficult obstacles to overcome, not only for the individuals but for society. The fixed mindset must be changed to a growth mindset of opportunity and making a positive difference not only in their lives but the lives of their children. Positive motivational influence is a primary source to initiate change. Presently, the incarcerated adult learner has several motivating factors or reasons for taking educational classes. One motivating mindset factor is that the individual has been court-ordered to participate in classes; another is to indicate to the parole board that they are attempting to reeducate themselves. Knowing the past and present mindset of the incarcerated individual is vital to the importance of this study to offer solutions for positive rehabilitation back into society. The mindset of the incarcerated individual must be changed from self-centered to family centered.

The adult incarcerated learner is motivated for self-improvement to obtain a better lifestyle by getting a job. This a self-centered approach and, according to Daniel Pink, is an approach that is flawed due to the desire of an individual to be "autonomous, self-determined, and connected to one another" (p.71). One of the basic themes established by the participants was the desire or need to belong or be loved, a desire that was never fulfilled. According to the women, the focus of education is self-centered so one can get a job and achieve success in a career path. The confusion is that most of the inmates while in school did not know what they wanted to do or even if it was possible in their neighborhoods. In the area of motivation and purpose, Daniel Pink states that "Autonomous people working towards mastery perform at very high levels. But those who do so in the service of a greater objective can achieve even more" (p. 131).

In the beginning of every new class, I ask the inmate-students what their purpose is for wanting to get a GED or HiSET diploma (see appendix E). The typical answer is to make it easier to get a job when released. This is a self-centered approach and based on their present needs. I also ask them questions about their values, goals, and dreams. Unfortunately, the answers are based on the norms of their family, community, peers, and school. The responses establish a sense of "who am I, where am I going, and how am I going to get there" based on the instituted norms of their society. I ask the students at what cost and how much pain had their criminal behavior affected them. The typical answer was incarceration. These answers were self-centered and the pain of their children, family, and friends did not enter into the responses. We further discussed cause and effect of their actions by focusing on the family and children. What was the cost of your actions, and how much pain did it cause your children and family? Separation from their children was the hardest, and that was the most painful result. How much pain did it cause for your children? The motivating factors to initiate change is not only for themselves but their children. This became the motivating factor to be more than self-centered, the desire to expand for the welfare of others, thus beginning to change the mindset of purpose.

At the last session, I ask the question, "What is your purpose now?" The mindset of the incarcerated student became not for oneself but to try to make sure their children did not follow them into prison. Their mindset toward education also changed from one of being forced to attend to one of realizing the importance of continuous learning so they can become a role model for their children by not focusing on the past but on the future. The motivational factors are changing from self-centered to a thought process of "I can make a difference" is not an easy task, especially when one's environment has been a self-centered survival mentality. Training is a necessity to succeed, but there are more difficulties and originally perceived. The mindset has to change from one of despair to one of hope. The role of the instructor is not only to instruct but to establish a level of confidence in the mindset of the students that they can succeed. In order to accomplish this task, motivational theories were included in the thought process and as a source for continuous professional development opportunities.

The foundation of initiating change must utilize motivational theories of learning. Fundamental sources are Allan Wigfield and Jacquelynne S. Eccles articles "Expectancy-Value Theory of Achievement Motivation" and "Motivational Beliefs, Values, and Goals" (p. 68). To achieve success, administrators must first address the present organizational structure and offer a solution to develop a better learning environment by giving the student a reason to learn and the confidence that they can learn. The expectancy-value theory was used to develop a coalition of collaborative support between the students and the instructor. The students began to feel that they were important and that they had a more important role than just getting an education. Their purpose became the welfare of their children. The theories on reason for engagement dealing with competence, expectancy, beliefs, goals, values became an important tool in developing the instructional format of the classroom setting in the jail facility.

As instructors, we had to present intrinsic motivation by developing enjoyment, using analogies that the student can relate to, and creating a sense of purpose far beyond the self. By incorporating intrinsic motivational techniques into the classroom, students began to develop self-determination skills by utilizing the theory that humans are motivated by stimulation and achieving competence. Csikszentmihalyi (1990) defined intrinsic motivation as totally engaged in an activity and labeled his theory as the "flow." Individuals are emotionally engaged in an activity. The extrinsic motivation of getting a reward is important to achieve recognition not only for themselves but also for the family to be aware of the accomplishment. The dream of the students was to make their children proud of their accomplishments, and graduating under prison conditions would send a message that if they could do it, their children could do it too. The girls realized that by setting goals and striving for the fulfillment of those goals, their purpose of to help and assist their children was also fulfilled.

Dale Schunk, in his book *Learning Theories as Educational Perspective*, writes about the importance of goals in in promoting self-efficiency and improved performance by reflecting on one's purpose (p. 135). Purpose is guided by values. The expectancy-value theory articulated by Eccles and Wigfield stipulates that there are values related to choices that have a cost to determine course of action or options. In actuality, theory was modified and based on "pain." How much pain did my previous actions cause, not only to me but my victims, my children, and my family? With this mindset of pain causation, the women had to ask themselves, "How much pain I will inflict if I proceed with certain actions?" Students who understand the cost or pain will attain the personal value of accomplishment and find self-worth. The emphasis of the self-worth theory is vitally important for the students to understand and appreciate. By establishing a positive self-image of self-worth, students are more apt to get out of their pseudo-safety zone and try new endeavors. Even though the women feel that they are labeled due to the criminal activity, the emphasis is on the future and not focused on the past. The women are told to use their past experiences as a positive tool by admitting "I messed up and have learned from my mistakes." Their value message is that if they can change, so can you.

Daniel Willingham, in his book *Why Don't Students Like School?* emphasizes the relationship between environment and memory. He concludes that educators "must ensure that students acquire background knowledge parallel with practical critical thinking skills" (p. 29). Social scientists must be cognizant of the environment from which the participant came from and utilize positive motivational skills to initiate change by developing purpose guided by values. By understanding environmental conditions and the importance of motivational theories, potential outcomes could have a positive impact on not just changing one person's life but changing a system from penance to rehabilitation and a mindset of continuous learning to help others. One participant mentioned that she wished the school taught to their needs and not the needs of suburbia.

Change the Mindset through Motivation

The mindset and motivation of prison practitioners is another contributing factor to the success or decline of the incarcerated individual. While it is clear the motivation and mindset influence learning experiences within the facility, it is the nature of educational programs within the public school system that must be addressed. Carol Dweck's book *Mindset: The New Psychology of Success* develops an insight as to the thought process of individuals and offers concepts on how to initiate change. Dweck emphasizes the importance differences between a fixed mindset and a growth mindset (pp.57–60). The fixed mindset student explains their failure by stating they are stupid or blaming someone else for their poor grades. The growth mindset personality developed curiosity and tried harder to use their failures as steppingstone to find the solution.

Further procedural expectations are to develop and understanding the nature of the narrative stories and initiate conversations for solutions to the problems. Marsha Rossiter argues in an article, "Possible Selves: An Adult Education Perspective" that learning "the concept of possible selves as a concept more closely related to the felt identity of persons. Possible selves refer to the future oriented components of the self-concept" (Rossiter 2007, 5). To change the mindset of the women, I incorporated the Don Miguel Ruiz's *The Four Agreements* as philosophy to follow in their daily lives (pp. 25–91).

1. Be impeccable with your words.
2. Don't take anything personally.
3. Don't make assumptions.
4. Always do your best and do more than what is expected.

Agreement 1 stipulates the use of impeccable words or words without sin. The Hitler analogy was used to explain on a broad scale the impact his peccable words had on the people of Poland prior to World War II and the Jews during the Holocaust. Ad hominem attacks without authenticity can destroy a person's life. Words have meaning and consequences. To personalize this first agreement, I asked the class if they have ever made a comment to an individual that was not true and was hurtful. The response was yes. I challenged the women to only use impeccable words so they can start to change their mindset from fixed to a growth mentality. Agreement 2 is about one's response to peccable words used against them. I tell the women that the person calling you names is using peccable words to get a reaction from you. How you react determines your fate. I asked them what they did when a situation occurred, and their response was to yell back or "beat the crap out of them." Both parties were using peccable words, and the situation escalated into a crisis of negative attitudes.

By not taking the words personally, the outcome of confrontation could have been avoided. I emphasized that they had to "walk the walk and not just talk the talk." This second agreement was difficult for some of the women due to the fact of their environment and image they felt they had to portray. The importance of this agreement was to change their mindset from one of confrontation to one of empathy and, by doing so, change the outcome to a positive occurrence. The third agreement of "don't make assumptions" was a process of changing the mindset of the women. I used the example of someone using nonverbal gestures or a strange glance, and you assume you know what they mean by their expression. In reality, the glance or expression might be something totally different from the manner you interpreted it. If there is a doubt about the meaning, ask for clarification and don't take it personally. If one assumes, the chances are that both parties will suffer the consequences.

The fourth agreement is extremely important in changing one's mindset, but more importantly, it will change the mindset of individuals judging you: the public school system, the women have been labeled as ignorant, angry, slow learners, gang members, and dysfunctional human beings. In the community, they have been labeled as criminals, jailbirds, and not desirable individuals. To prove them wrong, one must do more than what is expected. Even while incarcerated, the women have to do their best in following the rules by staying out of trouble. Once released from jail, it is difficult to find work. Often it takes weeks or months just to find a job. I tell the women that just doing what is expected is adequate, but if they want to advance their careers, they have to do more than what is expected.

I use the analogy of Michael Jordan as an example of doing more than what is expected. In Jordan's sophomore year in high school, he was cut from the varsity basketball team. Instead of quitting, he put in countless hours of practice over what was expected just to show the coaches that he had value. These four agreements are used to change the mindset of the individual and give them a course of action when facing adversity. The important aspect of these agreements are also tools the women can relate back to their children to help them change their mindset.

Summary

The implications of the cause of incarceration are as chaotic as the mindset of the individuals and situations or environment that put them in prison. If the mindset is not changed from a self-center survival mode to a family, community, and educational center, then the cycle will continue to be chaotic and self-destructive. Even though the implications are basically negative, there are opportunities to initiate change with positive implications of hope for the student inmates to have a positive impact on their families, communities, educational schooling, and most importantly themselves. The following chapter offers suggestions from the inmate students on how to initiate change. The format is to continue using Maslow's hierarchy of needs as a positive model to develop a solution to the obstacles that presently enslave the lives of the individuals.

CHAPTER 6

Inmate Solutions and Theory

The question should be if the hierarchy of needs was used for negative reactions, could the results be changed if the pyramid structure be applied in a positive manner? Throughout the course instruction and not for this research, the emphasis for the students have been individual responsibility for their actions and changing the mindset from self-centered to family- or children-centered. Their purpose is not to get an education so they can get a job but to become a role model for their children so their children do not follow them into the prison system. The students have become aware that their high school diploma can be a benchmark to show their children that success can be accomplished even in the harshest conditions of being confined to a jail cell. Maslow's hierarchy of needs was used as a guide for offering solutions not only for education but for the self, community, family, and peers. Other guidelines that were incorporated into the solution analysis were and Creswell's organizational structure and a revised Kotter's eight stages of creating change. The guidelines were introduced to the inmates to give them a foundation of knowledge to analyze and construct solutions.

Developing Positive Outcomes: Themes

Creswell's organizational structure of defining the setting or environment, identifying characters or individuals who have a narrative story, explaining the actions or behavior, describing the problems, and offering resolution that could initiate a solution to the research question (Creswell, p.511). I added another category to organize the story elements: Inmate Solutions for a Call for Action. The resolution element can be defined as a decree for action as prescribed by authoritative administrators. The reason for this additional element is to have the inmates be part of the solution by taking ownership in their decisions and be part of the transactional conversation, instead of receiving a linear directive.

Table 8. Problem Solution Narrative Structure
Organizing the Story Elements into the Problem Solution Narrative Structure

Settings	Characters	Actions	Problems	Resolutions
Context, environment, conditions, place, time, locale, year, and era	Individuals in the story described as archetypes, personalities, their behaviors, style, and patterns	Movements of individuals through the story illustrating the character's thinking or behaviors	Questions to be answered or phenomena to be described or explained	Answers to questions and explanations about what caused the character to change
Inmate Solutions for a Call for Action				

The format of this research offered clarification as to the environmental settings, the characters (including self), the actions or thought process, the problems that occurred due to that mindset, and answers for the actions taken. The additional element develops the importance of a collaboration of participants to determine a vision and/or strategy. The principles used to initiate positive outcomes are taken from John P. Kotter's books *Leading Change* (1996 and 2012), and as a course for action by using Creswell's organization structure. In order to initiate Kotter's eight-step approach, the motivation factors and changing the mindset of the individual has to be addressed first. By motivating and changing the mindset of the individual, the results will have a funnel-down effect on the family, community, peers, and the educational system. The student-inmates' first perception was not on the educational influences that influenced their criminal activity but their own behavioral patterns that led to incarceration. The funneling began with themselves by asking the basic questions of who am I, where am I going, and how am I going to get there? Kotter's eight stages helped them establish a sense of purpose and guided them with values that became a foundation for a positive change. Table 9 was used as a process to initiate change in their mindset toward themselves, family, peers, community, and education.

Table 9. Process of Creating Change
The Eight-Stage Process of Creating Major Change Source (adapted with permission from John P. Kotter, "Why Transformation Efforts Fail," *Harvard Business Review* (March-April 1995): 61)

1. Establishing a sense of urgency
   a) Examining realities
   b) Identifying and discussing crises, potential crises, or major opportunities

2. Creating a guiding coalition
   a) Putting together a group with enough power to lead the change
   b) Getting the group to work together like a team

3. Developing a vision and strategy
   a) Creating a vision to help direct the change effort
   b) Developing strategies to achieve vision

4. Communication the change vision
   a) Using every vehicle possible to constantly communicate the new vision and strategies
   b) Having the guiding coalition role model the behavior expected

5. Empowering broad based action
   a) Getting rid of obstacles
   b) Changing systems or structures that undermines the change vision
   c) Encourage risk taking and non-traditional ideas, activities, and actions

6. Generating short term wins
   a) Planning for visible improvements in performance or "wins"
   b) Creating those wins
   c) Visibly recognizing and rewarding people who made the wins possible

7. Consolidating gains and producing more change
   a) Using increasing credibility to change all systems, structures and policies
   b) Promoting, and developing people who can implement the change vision
   c) Reinvigorating the process with new projects, themes, and change agents

8. Anchoring new approaches in the culture
   a) Creating better performance through achievement orientated behavior
   b) Articulating the connection between new behavior and organizational structure
   c) Developing means to ensure family and community involvement

Self

The students individually wrote and collectively discussed the first of Kotter's eight stages by talking about the urgency by examining the realities of their situation by discussing the crises they face while being incarcerated. Some felt isolated from their family, especially from their children. Others felt shame for their criminal behavior and purposefully wanted to further isolate themselves from their family. They openly discussed the environment that they lived in and the reason for their criminal behavior. These discussions led to the questions of who am I, where am I going, and how will I get there? The main question asked was, what is my purpose? In actuality, the class became a coalition of support for one another and started to develop Kotter's second stage by developing a team mentality with the mindset that "I cannot do it myself, I need help to change from a negative to a positive force." The class talked about the urgency of their situation, and they developed a coalition of support for one another. By doing so, they began to develop the foundation for Maslow's hierarchy of needs. The jail facility provided the shelter, food, etc., but only on an individual basis, and does not meet the basic needs, such as supplying enough toilet paper. The class began to fulfill a positive identity as a group, and they began to help protect one another in the unit by defending one another. They even rationed toilet paper to the coalition, and indirectly, their behavior became a role model for other inmates.

Foundation for Developing Self Solutions

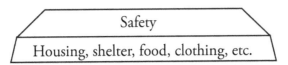

Figure 24. First Two Stages of Maslow's Hierarchy of Needs

Figure 24 shows the importance of developing a coalition of support in determining a self-course of action in collaboratively discussing problems and opportunities. The next stage is to establish a vision and strategies to enhance the individual's process of defining self-solutions. The class talked about the problems of self-identity as an incarcerated individual and came up with strategies that their criminal behavior could be used as a positive in defining who they really are. They talked about the importance of admitting that they were wrong in their behavior and wanted people, especially their children, to know that one has to take responsibility for one's actions. The importance of this admission is that they admit that they messed up, but they were determined to change their mindset to offer a positive solution for others to follow. The first strategy was to establish a vision of what they can do to improve their lifestyle, but more importantly, improve the mindset of their children. That became their goal. Instead of having a self-centered purpose, their purpose became family-oriented. The strategies used were to become a positive role model by communicating through their behavior and actions that even under the harshest conditions, positive attributes can be initiated to promote a change. The question became *how* do we communicate our new behavior?

The coalition talked about how one communicates to their children and to the family the importance of developing positive behavioral patterns. This is the fourth stage of Kotter's guidelines for initiating change and the further development of Maslow's hierarchy of needs. The class talked about telling the truth to their children of why they were incarcerated. This was a difficult decision that the women had to make. Some of the women told their children that they joined the military and would be away for a long period of time; others mentioned that they were relocated due to a business expansion. The consensus became that they had to tell their children the truth now or suffer the consequences later for lying and sending the message that it is okay to be untruthful. Tell your children that you are okay and that you are not in a nice place, but you will survive so the family can be back together. Send the message that there are consequences for one's actions.

The next phase of communication was to walk the walk and not just talk it. They talked about what kind of messages they should send to their family and children. The first message was to tell them that they are loved and that their children's welfare is the most important concern for them. Tell them that even though they are not there, other family members will take care of them. Give them a paper heart or other symbol of your love to remind them that every day you are thinking of them. Talk to them on the phone and listen to them by showing that you care for what they are doing. Most importantly, ask for forgiveness, but only after you have earned the right by having your family and children acknowledge that you are trying to change.

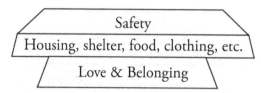

Figure 25. First Three Stages of Maslow's Hierarchy of Needs

The accomplishment of the first three sections of Maslow's hierarchy of needs and using Kotter's stages of development develops the next stage of being a risk taker, and using nontraditional thinking, the class began to establish a new self-esteem and self-actualization that change in mindset is possible. The fifth stage is empowering a broad base for action with nontraditional thinking and the confidence to be a risk taker in developing a new course of action. The prison system is a difficult place to initiate change, especially when communication is extremely linear and not transactional. Inmates are told when they can talk, when they can eat, and when they can sleep. Critical thinking or questioning authority is not permitted. Even among inmates, it is difficult to have a discussion or disagreement without someone taking it personally, which could threaten the hierarchy of the system. This coalition became a new factor in the unit and for the class: a coalition of support. Even when an individual was threatened by an individual not in the class, the coalition offered support. This new collaborative support group began to think outside of the traditional incarcerated mindset and became a positive role model for others to follow.

Even the jail official began to recognize the importance of this group by giving them special privileges because of their positive attitudes. They allowed extra pens and highlighters, extra essay books, and file folders, and they encouraged group-tutoring sessions within the unit. The guards even allowed class members to attend special counseling sessions before the class started. The ability to positively initiate change helped develop an attitude that one can make a difference, thus developing an attitude that they can be a positive force, even while being incarcerated. To keep the momentum going, Kotter suggests that there has to be rewards or short-term wins. The primary win for the class was that they created better communication with their family and children.

In the academic aspect, they created wins by studying hard and passing formative assessments that eventually will lead to the completion of the HiSET degree. The other win came from the recognition from other inmates that they could see a change in the attitude of the class members. The guards also recognized the class achievements, and one of the class members became a unit leader. Through these achievements, Kotter's seventh and eight stages are incorporated into the process by consolidating the gains and anchoring them as a format to continuously initiate change. The process helps fulfill Maslow's hierarchy of needs by giving the classmates the confidence and tools to change their mindset from self-centered to a greater-than-self way of life. They recognized that they "messed up," and they are willing to suffer the consequences. They came to the realization that they can still make a positive contribution to the lives of their children, family, peers, community, and hopefully to the educational system. They came to realization that they cannot do it themselves but need help from others.

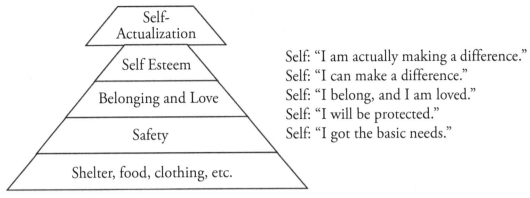

Figure 26. Hierarchy of Needs: Fulfillment of the Needs, Self

The significance of one initiating the positive change in the self is the first step in initiating change in the family, among peers, the community, and in the educational system. The women came to the realization that they can change their mindset and become a role model for others to follow. Even behind bars, they can have a tremendous impact on their family.

Family

The families of the incarcerated women are generally dysfunctional and had a significant role in criminal behavior and activities. The majority came from a single parent environment where the parental figure had also been incarcerated, or they were overly involved with the survival of the family and did not give special attention to the needs of their children. The women stated that a single parent can be a loving and supportive provider, but it was a difficult task to do without support from a husband or other family members. By using the accomplishments of the "self," the women felt it was imperative to use the same procedures used to assist the family in changing their mindset. They came to the realization that the first and foremost concern was the welfare of their children. Did the home that the children were living in offer the basic needs of shelter, food, clothing, etc.? Was the environment safe and secure, and was it a place that the children felt loved and respected? Were the children encouraged to dream, set goals, and were they rewarded for accomplishing their dreams and goals? If not, then Creswell's analyzation of the narrative, and Kotter's stages must be used to initiate change in the families' mindset. The women came to the realization that if the family was not willing to change, then they had to replace the existing family with a family that would offer a structure of support and encouragement based on Maslow's hierarchy of needs.

One of the members of the class asked to have her children put in foster care. The women knew about the conditions of the family structure and wanted to offer their support in initiating a positive change and, by doing so, helping their children and also with the family. They opened the dialogue by stating there was a sense of urgency in the environmental conditions and that she wanted to help. The women started to talk about the welfare of their children to other family members, including their spouse, parents, and grandparents. Thus, they began to develop a coalition that began to strategize a vision of support and guidance. The first strategy became the importance of education and helping the children succeed in school.

One woman had her parents order books for the children, and then they would have a discussion on the topic during phone conversations and during visitation. The first book that was ordered was *The Four Agreements* by Don Miguel Ruiz, and that book became the guideline for initiating a new mindset not only for the children but for the family. Another woman who had a third grade reading comprehension increased her scores to a ninth grade level in four months by motivating herself so she could read to her grandchildren. She wanted to become a role model by showing that when put to the challenge of focusing on the welfare of her grandchildren, great barriers could be overcome. The strategy for the family became the educational welfare of the children, and the women became the leading force in initiating change, thus developing the hierarchy, not only for the family but for themselves.

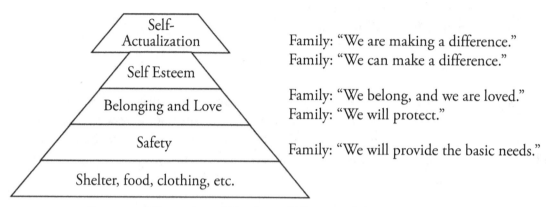

Figure 27. Hierarchy of Needs: Fulfillment of the Needs, Family

The solution for the family was to become a coalition of support with the vision to help the children in their educational needs. In reality, this is a difficult task due to the makeup of the families. Parents and grandparents had to be involved and motivated to ensure the importance of education for the children. In some cases, nontraditional thinking and risk taking became a format to initiate the change in the mindsets of the family. The norm was not reading or discussing books or homework, but this had to change. Rewards were given to the children for accomplishing certain goals, such as homework and getting better grades. Discussion about one's purpose, passion, and values were talked about and the importance of making the right decision. The guideline for decision-making for the children was how much pain would their actions cause if the wrong decision was made. Even though this barometer was used for the children, it also planted seeds in everyone's mind.

The solution to the family is a difficult task and includes more than just the welfare of the children. The environment of the living conditions is a major factor in determining the mindset of the individuals. Most of the men and women came from an impoverished neighborhood of low-income or subsidized housing. One of paroled men moved in with his brother who was an alcoholic and lived in their deceased parents' home. The home was in disrepair, and the yard was full of weeds, and the bushes were overgrown. The entire neighborhood was also in the same condition with litter, broken bottles, junk cars, and crime was rampant. In the class that Paul attended, we talked about how we are the message and that people interpret who we are by our looks, actions, and the environment that we live in. He cleaned up the yard, trimmed the bushes, planted flowers, and swept the street in front of the house. He took pride at what he had done to improve the living conditions, and his brother became more active in keeping the house clean and organized. His actions caused an unexpected response when the neighbors and his brother's friends complimented them on the home improvement.

Peers and Community

What started as self-improvement led to have a positive impact on the family and eventually with one's peers and the community. Some of the families of the women organized a coalition of other families to discuss problems facing the children. One woman mentioned that due to the crime in her neighborhood, her parents helped organize a coalition of mothers to walk their children to school as a group. This simple procedure led to socialization and conversations on how to improve the welfare of the children and the community. There was a sense of urgency, and the families developed a coalition that talked about strategies to improve the welfare of the children. This included the academic achievement of the children. The group communicated the need for academic assistance, especially in math, due to the lack of understanding the common-core methodology. They set up study sessions with their children and became risk takers by not using the common-core math format and reverted to the traditional teaching methods that they were taught in school. One of the inmates told me that her mother had her children memorize the multiplication tables, which helped her children not only with multiplication but also division. Another family started to share books with other parents. The outcome is unknown, but the foundation for academic improvement has been laid, and the families are feeling a sense of accomplishment.

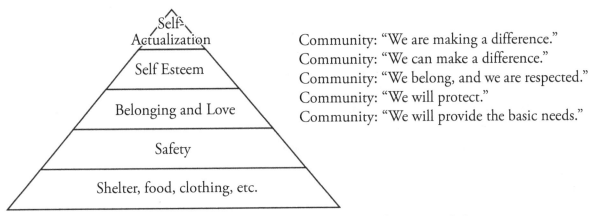

Figure 28. Hierarchy of Needs Fulfillment of the Needs, Peer, and Community

The story of Paul is how one individual can have a positive effect on not only himself but his family, his peers, and the community. When he was released from prison, he realized that he had to change his mindset from being fixed and accepting things the way they are to a growth mindset to initiate change. His actions by cleaning up the family house, planting flowers, and sweeping the street of broken glass caused both negative and positive reactions. At first, individuals kept throwing bottles and littering in front of his house. This could have been a negative reaction by individuals wanting to make a statement that this is "our turf." The positive reaction came from neighbors who also started to clean up their own properties. A coalition was developed, and strategies for a vision started to immerge. Paul was asked to help with the landscaping, and a growth mindset started to change the thought process of his neighbors. Littering became less frequent, and the police began to patrol the area more frequently. The people of the community became risk takers, and with the help of the police, they forced a "crackhouse" to leave the area. The Maslow hierarchy of needs and the Kotter's eight-stage process were used as guidelines for not only the self and family but also the community, including peers, to improve their positive action-orientated thought process. The main question asked to the class was about solutions for educational reform. The response was that before education can be reformed, self-image, the family structure, and the communal environment must be addressed to offer a foundation for acceptance to the importance of education.

Inmates Hierarchy for Education Solutions

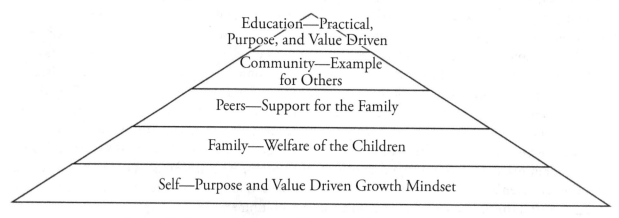

Figure 29. Process to Initiate Change in the Education System

In essence, the women and men developed a new hierarchy for the improvement of the educational system based on purpose and values of the self, family, peers, community, and educational support. The foundation of this new hierarchy became the self and the mindset for the welfare of their children. The women were originally self-centered for their own welfare, but after discussing the importance of the welfare of their children, their purpose became to prevent their children from also being incarcerated and going through the same pain that they have encountered. They emphasized the importance of education and stipulated problems, but also offered solutions.

Education

The primary research question is an inmate's perception of public education and the influence on criminal activity. The inmate-students initially blamed the educational system for a lot of their problems with criminal activity, but after analyzing their actions, they developed an attitude of self-responsibility. They also stipulated that the educational system did not offer support or guidance, even when they were silently asking for help. Throughout this research, I asked the students what the problems with their educational experience were and if their children are facing the same experiences. Their answers are summarized from the questionnaire, focus group, interviews, and classroom discussions. The most common perceptual answers were the following:

Perceived Problems of Public-School Education

1) School is boring.
2) Teachers did not care.
3) They just passed me on.
4) They never told me why I had to learn math or history.
5) They just lectured to us and told us to learn this without explaining *why*.

6) Gangs and peer pressure.
7) The school could not relate to my needs.
8) They never told me that if I did not learn to read by the third grade, I would have difficulty with all of my subjects and be left behind.
9) They never had me set goals or even tell me to dream about what I want to do.
10) They never listened to me; just told me what to do, how to act, and what to learn.
11) My eleven-year-old had to teach her cousin how to read and write in cursive.
12) Common core made learning more difficult, and I cannot even explain it to my children, who are also struggling.
13) The school gave me no purpose or values when I was hoping that they would since I did not get them from anywhere else.

The last answer was the most disturbing because it indicated a much larger problem than just the school system. These were the basic answers to the problems facing the inner-city students. As a researcher, I realize that there is a difference between inner-city and suburban school districts, and maybe their answers reflect why there is a large academic achievement gap and the grade-level equivalency among the inmate students. The answers reflect a sense of urgency, and with problems, there becomes opportunities to initiate change. The next question I asked was for their ideas on how to improve the educational system. The discussions were held during the Friday morning classroom sessions during October of 2018. Their answers are recorded below and their answers were transcribed from my notes and discussed with the students for clarification and accuracy in November 2018.

Student Inmates' Solutions to Public-School Education

1) Listen to us even when we are not talking and don't be afraid of us.
2) Explain to us the purpose and value of education and don't tell us it is to get a job. There is more, like having us set goals and dreams, encouraging us to follow our passions, giving us hope and confidence that we can succeed.
3) Don't teach us the way they do in suburban schools. We are inner city with different cultures, languages, and survival needs. Teach us by relating to our needs. Get rid of common core and teach us in the more traditional way.
4) Stop testing to the test and not the subject matter that is relevant to the student's needs. Use the tests as a learning tool for the final examination, but don't penalize the students who fail the initial test but finally grasp the concepts at the end of the semester.
5) Don't just pass a student on to the next grade if they don't understand the course material. In the long run, having them repeat will benefit them more than just passing them on.
6) More one-on-one tutoring. If the teachers don't have the time, then have students who understand the subject matter tutor us. Take fifteen minutes of the class period and have students work together explaining the problem and solution.
7) Different classes for different levels of understanding. Integrate with everyone, but still have special classes for people who need extra assistance. Offer more AP classes for students who are motivated to learn.
8) Reading, history, and math tests—and I don't know what they are talking about. Make it more relational to what we know.
9) Curriculum for suburbia is taught in the inner city. Hard to relate.

10) It wasn't the school. I was too busy trying to fit in, smoking the weed. The problem I had with science is that I could not relate to what they were talking about.

11) Get students' opinions on how to learn. No feedback from students. Don't just lecture to us, get us involved with discussions and our opinions.

12) Get students, parents, community and business leaders, gangs, teachers, and administrators involved in designing the needs of the students and not just have administrators telling us what we have to do. Also have the coalition help design the "norms or expectations" of the students so everyone takes ownership in the process.

13) Longer school hours that meet the needs of the parents. Don't dismiss school early when the parents' work is not dismissing them.

14) Teach us values and that there are consequences for our actions. Use Toltec's agreements as a guideline for our behavior: (1) impeccable words, (2) don't take it personally, (3) don't assume anything, (4) do your best or more than what is expected, and (5) be skeptical and learn to listen. *We are not getting it anywhere else.*

15) Have the parents be involved with disciplinary actions, even requiring the parents to go to school and attend classes with their child.

16) Put more emphasis on vocational training. Not everyone is going on to college. Have certificate programs for hairstyling or construction work or truck driving. If I had the skills to be a hairdresser, then maybe I could have gotten a job right out of school and not landed up in jail.

17) Have teachers become more aware of different learning styles.

18) Have students who cannot speak English learn English first before being put into a traditional classroom. Helps the teachers and the student by not having to translate instructions from English to their language and back again.

19) Teach us how to use information technology and not just for social media.

20) Get rid of cell phones in the classroom.

21) Teach us to be nontraditional thinkers, to be risk takers, to be curious, to be creative, to be entrepreneurs, and to think outside of the box.

22) Have teachers take classes on how to motivate students.

23) Have teachers take anger management classes and ask the question why we behave the way we do.

24) Have teachers make us feel that we are important.

25) Get rid of teachers who cannot teach.

26) If you do what you've always done, that's what you will be.

Throughout the conversations about solutions to the educational system in the public schools of the inner city, the students offered insights as to what should be done to improve the system. Their answers reflect an attitude based on their own experiences and the experiences that their children are presently going through. Their answers also reflect an attitude that they wished they could have had when they were in school. It became apparent that Maslow's hierarchy of needs was the format to improve the system: "Provide us with the basic needs, give us a safe environment, make us feel that we belong, help us achieve knowledge so we can reach our potential, and help us gain self-worth."

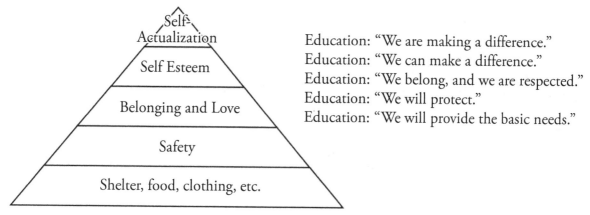

Figure 30. Hierarchy of Needs: Fulfillment of the Needs, Education

The students used Kotter's eight stages in *Leading Change* to format solutions for the continuous improvement of the educational system. They stipulated that there were problems with the public school system in the inner city and almost demanded changes to be made for the welfare of their children. The sense of urgency is now. In the conversations, they stated the importance of developing a coalition of parents, community leaders, media, gang members, educators, and students to develop strategies and a vision for improving the educational system, so everyone takes ownership in the decisions. By bringing all the factions of society into the coalition, they developed a format of communication so everyone could be informed about the progress.

The students have become risk takers by their suggestion of inviting gang members into the coalition. This nontraditional thinking of allowing all aspect of the community to be part of the solution could become a cornerstone for further involvement in creating a positive change in the traditional educational thought process. A short-term win could be the recognition by the school administration of the importance of involvement of all interested parties, including the students in developing "norms and expectations." Another win could be the establishment of a coalition of teachers to discuss the problems facing the students and come up with positive enhancements to teaching methodology and curriculum design. The consolidation of the gains made by various coalitions could become the anchor to initiate change in the educational culture as a process to be continuously used.

Reciprocal Evolution Theory for Educational Improvement

The themes that developed from this research ranged from the dysfunctional family, the destruction of the individual through the lack of self-worth, peer pressure not to succeed, lack of an inclusive and progressive community organization, and the disillusionment of the purpose of education—all leading to a fixed mindset of no hope or opportunity to change the inmate-student's life conditions. When there are problems addressed and a sense of urgency developed, the inmates came up with solutions to the various segments of society that have been instrumental in their own downfall. Maslow's hierarchy of needs was used as a foundation to help develop their own self-actualization and the actualization of the other segments. Kotter's adapted eight stages in *Leading Change* were used as a guideline for self-improvement to initiate change in the mindset from fixed to growth.

The themes of destruction also developed a theory for positive change in the various different segments to improve the educational system in the inner city. The reciprocal evolution theory for educational improvement was developed by the inmates to insure continuous improvement of programs that are beneficial to all concern. The premise is that from the mindset of the incarcerated student, their purpose must change from self-centered to a mindset of benefiting others, especially their children. The guiding force for this change in mindset is the amount of pain one causes by the decisions they make and the benefits or rewards that occur from their actions. The students paraphrased *The Prayer of Jabez* by Bruce Wilkinson and used it to give them inspiration to initiate change (2002, 92).

The Prayer of Jabez

> And Jabez called on the God of Israel saying, "Oh, that you would bless me indeed, and enlarge my territory, that your hand be with me, and that you would keep me from evil, that I may not cause pain!" So God granted what her requested. (1 Chronicles 4:10 NKJV)

The students could relate to this Bible verse because of the decisions they have made and their desire to live a more meaningful life not only for themselves but for their children. Jabez in Hebrew is interpreted as a word that caused distress or pain, and they could relate because they caused so much pain not only in their lives but in the lives of their family, victims, and community. They came to the realization that they could not continue on in their present mindset but needed help from others to change to a more positive and productive lifestyle. The student-inmates felt it was their responsibility to start the process of initiating change in their own thought process, which would influence the other segments of the thematic problems. Maslow's hierarchy of needs was used as a guide to format the process of change. Their primary focus became their family, especially their children, which would have an influence on peer groups, community, and a positive reaction from education. The students also felt that if they could not get assistance from the family, peers, or community, then it had to be the responsibility of the educational system to assist them by developing an innovative curriculum and communicating the rewards and benefits to the other segments, thus making the process a reciprocal evolution.

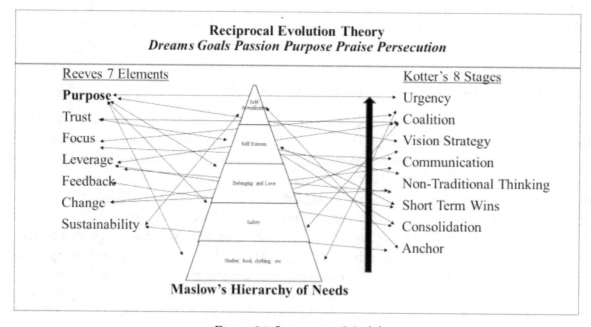

Figure 31. Interactive Model

The reciprocal evolution theory is based on an interactive approach by leadership to ensure all participants are involved by taking ownership in the decisions that directly affect their situation. It is a bottom-up approach that can be used by the self, family, peers, community, and especially by educational leadership as a model to initiate change.

Table 10. The Reciprocal Evolution Theory for Educational Improvement

Education	Education	Education	Education	Self	Maslow's
Community	Peers	Family	Self	Family	Self-Actual
Peers	Community	Self	Family	Peers	Self-Esteem
Family	Self	Community	Peers	Community	Belonging
Self	**Family**	**Peers**	**Community**	**Education**	Safety
					Physiological

The reciprocal evolution theory for educational improvement is based on the life experiences of the incarcerated student and on reflections of "who am I, where am I going, and how will I get there." Initially, the question that frustrated the students was what their "purpose" was, but after reflecting on the three basic questions of self-identity, their purpose became greater than self. The inmates' theory is based on adaptions of Maslow's hierarchy of needs, Kotter's *Leading Change*, and Douglas Reeves's *From Leading to Succeeding: Seven Elements of Effective Leadership* as formats to sustain their own new mindset and also the mindset of the other segments of the study. Other concepts mentioned in chapter 2 are mentioned in chapter 7 to offer clarification and guidance to initiate change in an educational experience.

Summary

The students indicated that throughout this chapter, there are many facets to the problems facing their survival. Education alone is not the problem, but the other elements of society contribute to educational neglect. The family structure has to be improved from being dysfunctional to a positive unit of support and guidance. Peers and community must have a purpose of offering solutions to the difficulties facing the individual. Educational schooling must be willing to offer programs that meet the needs of the individual and the community. There has to be a collaborative effort between all segments in order to achieve academic excellence by developing a sense of purpose guided by common values. The inmate-students felt the most important aspect was for them to change their mindset from being self-centered to a greater need for others. The gauge they are using is the amount of pain and rewards their decisions are creating. The reciprocal evolution theory for educational improvement is continuously evolving from one segment to another, which could be detrimental or beneficial to all concerned individuals or organizations.

CHAPTER 7

Reflection and Conclusion

I have learned that success is to be measured not so much by the position that one has reached in life as by the obstacles he has overcome while trying to succeed. (Booker T. Washington, *Up from Slavery*, 24)

Researcher Reflections

The quote from Booker T. Washington is a message that even though one has suffered from misdeeds and hardships, it does not mean that one cannot succeed. This was the message that I wanted to present to the women. As a researcher, it was hard to comprehend the crimes the women committed. I knew what they did and how they did it, but I had to find out the *why* of their actions and did their educational experience have any influence on their criminal activity. In order to understand the why and to collectively come up with solutions, I used the Johari window as a format to understand myself and to begin a process of self-disclosure of myself and from the women. The Johari window was used as a learning device and as a format for the students to learn from others by giving them a chance to listen, to observe, and not to prejudge. The window is divided into four quadrants of openness, hiddenness, blindness, and unknown and is a training tool for understanding the need and purpose of disclosure.

Table 11. Self-Reflection and Understanding Others: Johari Window

	Known to Self	**Unknown to Self**
Known to Others	Open: Aspect of self that you and others are aware of and you are willing to self-disclose	Blind: What is apparent to others that you do not think they know
Not Known to Others	Hidden: Things that you are aware of, but do not want others to know	Unknown Opportunities: Self-discovery through self-reflection by observing consistent patterns in one's behavior

(McCornack, 58–59)

From the researcher perspective, in the beginning of this project, the open area or quadrant for the inmate students was extremely small, and it could have been the same scenario when they were in school. At the first meeting, the women were skeptical and not sure of the purpose of this class and did not disclose much personal information. They were all dressed in orange or yellow jumpsuits, wore slippers, and some had tattoos. Some acted as if they were tough and others scared of being in the jail environment and not knowing what to disclose in front of other inmates. Some were skeptical of another jail program, and in order to eliminate this skepticism, I had to begin the process by self-disclosing who I was and what were my motives and intentions. I told them that I did not care about their past or the crimes they committed, but I really cared about their future, and I wanted to give them an opportunity to initiate change in their thought process. My next statement expanded greatly my open window by asking the women if they would participate in a research project that could offer an insight to the reason of why and maybe offer solutions to prevent others from getting involved in criminal activity.

Table 12. Johari Window Results

	Known to Self	Unknown to Self		Known to Self	Unknown to Self
Known to others	Open	Blind	→	Open	Blind
Not known to others	Hidden	Unknown		Hidden	Unknown

Initially, I asked the women basic questions: What is your name? Where did you grow up? Do you have any children? The responses were very short and direct: name, location, and yes, I asked them how many children. Of the fifteen participants, thirteen had children ranging from the ages of one to twenty-six. Their open window began to expand, and the hidden quadrant started to become smaller. The benefit to these questions were that the women started to realize that they were not alone and that other inmates had similar backgrounds. The next question I asked was pertaining to purpose. "What is your purpose for taking the HiSET class?" The answer was universally the same. "So I can get a job to support myself." This answer was generally very "self-centered," but over the next few sessions, the answer started to change. I asked them about how much pain they caused not only to themselves but to their children, family, and to their victims. I also was able to ask them what they told their children of why they were not at home with them.

One woman mentioned that she was on an extended business trip and another said she told her children that she was in the army serving overseas. The class began using the Kotter's eight stages as a guide to come up with solutions. The class felt that there was a problem with some of the answers of why they were away. The class became a coalition of support that came up with strategies to answer that particular question. The strategy was to tell the truth and to admit that they did something wrong and now had to suffer the consequences. The reason for this strategy was the question of what the consequences would be when their children found out the truth and the benefits for telling the truth. By communicating with their children, they sent a message that lying was wrong and that eventually the lie would come back and cause mistrust.

After I felt that the women's open window had begun to expand and that they were comfortable with disclosure, I asked them about the structure of their family. I started the conversation using Maslow's hierarchy of needs as a guide for conversation and also a format to motivate themselves. The physiological needs were discussed to develop a foundational process for discussion and to have the women reflect on their experiences and the present situation with their children. The next two levels of the pyramid related to the safety and belonging that the women experienced and then asked to compare those experiences to the lifestyle of their children. The purpose was to see if there was a pattern, and I reminded them that when asked if either of their parents had been incarcerated, their answer was *yes*. I restated the statistic that 71 percent of the children of incarcerated parents will also be incarcerated. By examining the basic levels of the hierarchy, the women's thought process of being "self-centered" began to change to a purpose of developing a more efficient hierarchy for their children.

Self-Worth

By reflecting on the basic questions of who am I, where am I going, and how am I going to get there? the women's mindset started to change from the "self" to the welfare of others, especially their children. They used the hierarchy of their children's needs to initiate their own self-esteem and self-worth by being determined to facilitate the well-being of their children. They felt that even being incarcerated, they could still have a positive impact on not only the children but also the family, peers, community, and the educational system. Bandura further explains in *Self-Efficacy: The Exercise of Control,* the importance of learning in that "students' self-efficacy beliefs influence their performance in several ways. It is a consistent predictor of their pursued course of action, coping behaviors (i.e., effort, persistence, and resilience), and ultimately, their achievements" (1997, 43).

According to Bandura, learning is a four-step process of attention, retention, production, and motivation. (1997, 89). The attention process is the functionality or value of instruction. The retention process is the cognitive capabilities to further retain the functional value of educational learning. The production process allows for a course of action, and the motivational process is the self-efficacy or self-actuation that the individual has value and a purpose. The course design allowed the women to work together as a coalition of support and that they were not alone in their determination to develop a purpose beyond themselves, for others.

Four-Step Process

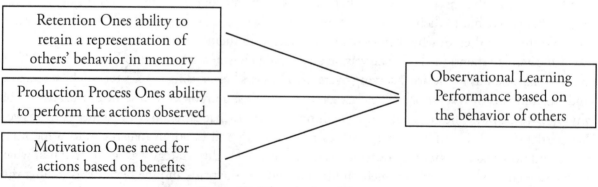

Figure 32. Observational Learning

The understanding of Bandura's theory on behavior change is vital to this study. Figure 30 shows the process of learning and how an individual's past experiences, the influence of peer behavior, social pressure, and the emotional state of the individual can determine the outcome of one's behavior (p. 195). Figure 24 shows the difficulties the women had in overcoming the lack of self-worth, especially in the family, peer, community, and educational environments that they had experienced. The jail or prison environment is not helpful in developing self-efficacy or worth. Inmates are told what to do, when to do it, and how to behave. This is understandable, but the structure must also offer opportunities for personal growth by offering to help develop a sense of purpose beyond getting a job and not committing crimes. The purpose- and value-driven format of the classroom became a model of Maslow's hierarchy of needs. There were the basic physiological needs provided by the county, and the classroom became a safety zone where the women felt comfortable expressing themselves beyond what was expected back in the pods or units. The women began to reflect on their past experiences and felt they belonged to a group of individuals who had experienced the same situations. More importantly, they began to develop a new mindset of self-importance by focusing on the needs of others instead of themselves.

Efficacy Expectations

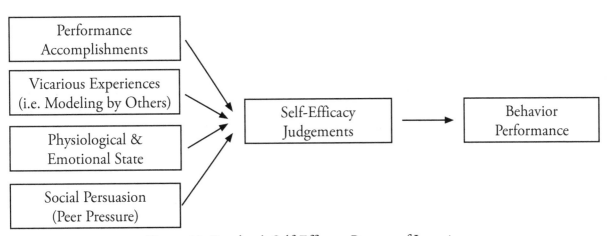

Figure 33. Bandura's Self-Efficacy Process of Learning

According to Frank Pajares in his paper "Gender and Perceived Self-Efficacy in Self-Regulated Learning," the beliefs students develop about their academic capabilities help determine what they do with the knowledge and skills they have learned: "Consequently, their academic performances are, in part, the result of what they come to believe they have accomplished and can accomplish" (p. 116). Bandura further supports Pajares's self-efficacy concept by defining self-efficacy as "the individual's perceived ability to succeed at or accomplish certain tasks." Self-efficacy or self-actuation is the motivating factor of finding benefits or rewards for the accomplishment of obtaining a sense of value and purpose. The motivational theories offer a format for self-efficacy that one's life expectations can be changed, and through the use of these theories, the women can change their perspective of their life and the lives of their children. School officials can use these theories to develop a coalition of collaborative support between the students and the instructor. The students can begin to feel that they are important and that they have a more important role in society. The theories on reason for engagement dealing with competence, expectancy, beliefs, goals, values must become an important tool in developing the instructional format of the classroom setting in the jail facility and in the public school system. The format is there for the women to develop a greater sense of self-efficacy or worth. They know why and what must to be done, but the frustration for the women is how they will do it.

Purposeful Change Guidelines

Their mindset began to change from being fixed to growth and a purpose of being a positive role model for the benefit of others, especially their children. To help facilitate this growth mindset, I incorporated Douglas Reeves's concepts from his book *From Leading to Succeeding: The Seven Elements of Effective Leadership in Education* and altered the elements, with his permission, so they can be applied as an intrapersonal format for the women to assist in redefining their own self-worth. The women had to dream and visualize the reward of this new growth mindset, and they had to establish achievable goals not only for themselves but also to communicate these seven elements to their children. The desire to make a difference in the lives of others became their "passion," which became their purpose.

Seven Elements of Effective Intrapersonal Achievements

Adapted with permission *From Leading to Succeeding: The Seven Elements of Effective Leadership in Education* by Douglas Reeves

1) *Purpose.* The women developed a clear and concise vision with a mission statement that collaboratively stated, "Believe in me so you can believe in yourself." Originally, the purpose of the women was to get a job, but now their purpose changed to the welfare of others, especially their children.

   The reason for this change was based on the amount of pain they had caused and their desire not to have their children have the same outcome as they were experiencing. Their purpose was to use the importance of education as a process to achieve self-esteem and potentially self-actualization of goals and dreams and to relay that message to their children. Their defined purpose of getting their HiSET diploma was a message to their children that even under the harshest conditions, one can still accomplish preestablished dreams and goals. By establishing their purpose, the women achieved a sense of self-esteem through the thought process of "I can make a difference in my own life but also have a positive influence on others."

2) *Trust.* Trust in oneself is the first step, then seeking trust in others. The women can be forgiven for many mistakes as long as their family trusts them—that what their new purpose is actually fulfilling.

   The statement of purpose must be followed through, or if changed, an explanation must be given as to the reason. Reeves stated that mistakes happen, and the trust factor is determined on how an individual resolves the situation. The women must be able to walk the walk and not just talk the talk. Forgiveness is the first step in developing trust with the family and children. One has to admit they did wrong and use those mistakes as examples for what not to do. Trust is built on many factors, including developing a coalition of collaborative participation so the whole system takes ownership. Trust is also built on short-term wins that indicate that the individual is actually making progress in initiating change in their attitude. These short-term wins could be as simple as consistently writing letters or talking on the phone and telling their children the accomplishments that they have made. The most important short-term win that will become long term is listening to their children and telling them that you love them. Building trust within the family is critical, but the women also need to build trust with their coalition of fellow inmates, and that can be as simple as saying, "Thank you for helping and keeping me focused on my mission."

3) *Focus.* Staying on course and not wavering from your purpose, goals, vision, and mission is not an easy task, but is mandatory for success in not only changing your life but the lives of others. Reeves stipulates that conscious leaders have choices on what they will do or will not do. Reeves uses the term *calendar integrity* as a term to help visualize the importance of their values and priorities (p. 31).

The focus must be on their purpose, mission, and vision of collaborative strategies of developing a positive message for the family and their continuing efforts to get their HiSET Diploma. I have told the women that by staying on course, they will accomplish greater rewards that, as of this time, they cannot even imagine. I also told them that getting the diploma could be one of the hardest tasks they have ever tried to accomplish. But once completed, it can never be taken away from them. By being focused on the mission, the message that is sent to the individual is that "I can achieve what I am seeking"; and more importantly, it is sending a message to their children the importance of establishing goals and being focused on accomplishing those dreams. Unfortunately, many of the women have had the mindset of taking the easy way out and not putting in the effort to study because they did not have a purpose or did not understand why they needed an education. There will be distractions, especially when the women are back in the unit or pod. They will be verbally attacked by others who have failed in school and do not want others to succeed. They have to remain focused on the outcome they want to fulfill and not to take the attacks personally because the other person is insecure in their own course of action and that they are speaking peccable or sinful words that are used to distract you from your mission. I remind the women that they are now on a journey and that there will be difficulties that will sidetrack them from fulfilling their mission, but they will have to constantly evaluate their decisions and remain focused on their mission. By remaining focused on the mission, the women will gain leverage not only with other inmates and educators, but will gain trust with themselves and their family.

4) *Leverage.* We believe in you. By accomplishing goals and tasks, one gains an advantage by being focused and trusted to fulfill a responsibility and to initiate other agendas; and through leverage, one can influence others through credibility.

Leverage from one's past accomplishments based on a purpose, trust, and a focused mission can influence others to believe in you when you offer new concepts to create a better environment not only for your family but for others including peers, community, and with educators. Leverage is gained by developing creditability or trust by offering new approaches to solve difficulties and making them opportunities.

One woman suggested to her son, who was struggling in reading about the American Revolution, that he visualize himself in the readings. She suggested that he even visualize himself wearing the same clothing and feel the coldness of the weather conditions when Washington crossed the Delaware. She even suggested that he was the one rowing the boat for General Washington. The following week, they talked about the ordeal, and her son said he was the best "bad-ass" rower in Washington's boat; and without him, they would have never got to the other side. She took it a step further by asking him what the significance of the encampment at Valley Forge was and that he had to do the research to find the answers. He told her that even though one is facing the harshest conditions, if one believes in the purpose, one can persevere and accomplish one's goals. Through her suggestion of visualization, she gained credibility with her son by offering a new technique to learning. More importantly, she gained respect by offering a different approach to learning. Being focused on task-orientated projects, adopting innovative approaches, and emphasizing the completion of the mission gains a leverage for the next situation of importance. In order to retain leverage, one must have positive and encouraging feedback that is constructive and meaningful.

5) *Feedback*. The leverage or credibility one gains can be quickly lost if informative feedback is not given in a proper timeframe or format.

Hattie and Yates (2014) identifies feedback as "one of the most powerful factors implicated in academic learning and resultant achievement" (2014, 68). Using the example of Valley Forge, the women had several conversations with her son and offered timely and positive feedback, but also asked him to tell her more. The outcome was that the son was excited to tell her that Valley Forge was the turning point in the American Revolution by making a ragtag army into a professional military force. Giving proper and timely feedback reinforced that the woman's purpose was partially being fulfilled and that she became trusted because of her empathy to listen and also learn from her son. Her feedback became encouragement, which helped facilitate the "art of leading change" in the mindset of her son and, more importantly, in her own mindset of self-worth. Positive, timely, and instructive feedback are important aspects to initiate change, but one has to realize, especially in the mindset of the women, that change is a difficult task. The women must have the attitude and the tools to realize that change is possible.

6) *Change*. The change element is what is needed to insure continuous learning and continuous improvement in the lives of the student inmates. The change element must be guided by dreams, visions, and goals with a sense of purpose. More importantly, change must be driven by values and "passion."

Change is not an easy task, especially for the women. They want to change their lifestyle but are unsure how to do it. Several of the women have been incarcerated more than once, and the question remains *why*. Most of the recidivism comes from the women going back into a dysfunctional environment that sent them to prison in the first place. In some cases, they felt more comfortable in a prison setting, with boundaries and a structure of being controlled with a mindset of accepting failure. As unfortunate as that may be, it is understandable due to the fact that they were never given the tools to succeed or the confidence that they could make a difference. They were never told to dream and establish goals or to follow their "passion." These attributes were never taught to them in the public school system, according to their responses to the original research question of influences to criminal behavior. Reeves established the guidelines by demanding the elements of purpose, trust, focus, leverage, feedback driven by "passion" so that change can be a positive experience—an experience that can lead to sustainability.

7) *Sustainability*. The importance of sustainability is that they endure and become a way of life and a process to fulfill one's sense of purpose and the purpose of other initiatives.

Sustainability is the process to anchor and develop new approaches into the culture of the organization (Kotter, 23). Reeves's six preceding elements are mandatory to successfully initiate programs for continuous improvement in an educational system. In order to help develop sustainability in a passion-driven purpose, there must be consistency and perseverance in every aspect of the elements and stages to effectively initiate change in the mindset of all concerned from the person delivering the message to the individuals receiving. Even though Kotter and Reeves used their concepts for effective leadership in business and education, this study used them to initiate change in the mindset of the individual student to sustain their purpose and vision for the welfare of their children, family, peers, community, and the educational system.

Reflection on Self, Family, Peers, Community, and Education

The primary research question was the influence of public education on criminal behavior, and initially their answers led to the conclusion that the public school educational system was a major cause of their criminal activities. The answers in the questionnaire and from the focus-group sessions led to that conclusion. The interviews also reflected that the educational system contributed to their criminal activities. The classroom discussions on the reasons of *why* started to initiate a different thought process and that the problem was just not the educational system but also included their own thought process, their dysfunctional family, peer-group influences, and negative attitude of their communities. In the classroom settings, I introduced Carol Dweck's Brainology concept that the more one challenges the mind to learn, brain cells begin to reform. I had them journal their problems and had also develop solutions to those difficulties (pp. 228–233). We talked about Shelby Steele and his book *The Content of Our Character* and how "there will be no end to despair and no lasting solutions to any of our problems until we rely on individual effort within the American mainstream" (p.173). I talked about the African American issue in our society, and then I replaced the word *Black* with *convict*. I emphasized that the content of their character was not their past but what they are doing now and what they will be doing in the future.

We talked about maybe our purpose was to be incarcerated so we can have a positive influence on the lives of others. The discussion led to Thomas Sowell's *external versus internal explanations* as a format to understand the importance of self-reflection, the importance vision, and the need for external assistance, but more importantly, the internal motivation and responsibility to initiate change (pp. 249–250). I use Anthony Muhammad's *Components of the Liberation Mindset* of equality, responsibility, and advocacy as a thought process for individual growth and achievement (pp. 94–102). I used the liberation mindset to "human potential is not a function of personal characteristics like race, gender, economic status, home language, national origin, or disability" as a reminder of individual responsibility (p.94). Daniel Pink in his book *Drive* offers an insight as to why individuals need to take charge of their own lives and offers a guideline to motivate oneself, not on being self-centered, but centered on the welfare of others, especially their children (p. 145).

Summary

In the fourth quadrant of the Johari window, the sustainability is still unknown. But the women are self-motivated to sacrifice their well-being for the well-being of their children and others. They are influenced by Reeves's seven elements, Kotter's eight stages, and Maslow's hierarchy of needs, which helped guide the women to expand their "open window" and close the "hidden." The "blind window" also changed by them allowing me to openly express to the women my feelings about their improvement and how they were beginning to answer the questions of who am I, where am I going, and how am I going to get there?

Conclusions

The focus of this research was an inquiry into the perceptions of inmates to their educational experiences and the influences it had on their criminal behavior. What started as a project to see if education had a role in criminal activity turned into a three-year course of personal growth of understanding and sense of accomplishment, not just for me but the men and women involved with this study. The initial findings from the questionnaire, focus-group sessions, and interviews were that the public school education had an influence on criminal behavior but were not the only factors. The dysfunctional family, peer-group interventions, and the lack of positive community organization also contributed to the individuals being incarcerated. The main finding from the classroom settings was that they themselves were the problem and that they had to take responsibility for their actions. The most rewarding aspect was that the women felt that they could also be part of the solution, not only with the family, peers, community, educational system, and also with themselves. It was their belief that they had to initiate the change in the mindset of all concerned parties.

The reciprocal evolution theory for the improvement of education became a reminder to us all that everyone must be involved in initiating change. The women wanted to start the process by planting seeds of change using the principles mentioned in this study. Even though there was a limited number of participants, the results indicated a need for reform in our inner-city public school system by including all aspect of society, including the students in the decision of the direction of education. By developing high standards, norms of behavior, and establishing a purpose and value-driven educational program, all segments of society will benefit. My hope is that school districts will do more research on purpose- and value-driven education by allowing all aspect of society to be involved. My hope is that the solutions presented by the inmates will be considered and discussed to further implement change in the system. My hope is that teachers and administrators, family members, peer groups, and community leaders realize that most of the incarcerated individuals did not want to be incarcerated but wanted positive guidance and hope for the opportunity to succeed. If the family, peers, and community could not lead the way, then it is mandatory for the school system, including the prison educational system, to initiate programs that serve the individual by giving them the opportunity to establish goals, to dream, and to develop self-efficacy by establishing a sense of purpose.

Further research is needed in areas of prison and educational reform. One research study would be the influence of prison personnel on criminal activity after an inmate is released from jail or prison. An inmate asked the question, "Will we treat people the same way guards treated us?" The same question can be asked of educators and their responsibility to instill a purposeful and value-driven educational program. These two additional studies should also offer solutions from the guards and from the teachers. To help verify the importance of the reciprocal evolution theory of education improvement, studies should be conducted of families, peers, and community to help clarify the role each segment has in developing an improved educational system. Another important study would be a comparison between inner city and suburban school districts. The research question could be the economic differences and the effectiveness of curriculum design in determining educational excellence and decreasing the academic achievement gap.

REFERENCES

Aizer, A., and Doyle, J. 2015. "Juvenile Incarceration, Human Capital, and Future Crime: Evidence from Randomly Assigned Judges." *The Quarterly Journal of Economics* 130, no. 2: 759–803.

Bandura, A. 1997. "Self-Efficacy: Toward a Unifying Theory of Behavioral Change." *Psychological Review* 84, no. 2: 191–215. doi: 10.1037/0033-295X.84.2.191.

———. 1997. *Self-Efficacy: The Exercise of Control.* New York: W. H. Freeman.

Baska, R. S. 2015. "Inmates' Attitudes Toward Pre-Release Educational and Vocational Programs." Department of Justice. https://files.eric.ed.gov/fulltext/ED560264.pdf.

Belfield, C., B. Bowden, A. Klapp, H. Levin, R. Shand, and S. Zander. 2015. *The Economic Value of Social and Emotional Learning.* New York: Center for Benefit-Cost Studies in Education Teachers College, Columbia University.

Bonnie, R. J. 2012. *Reforming Juvenile Justice: A Developmental Approach.* Washington, District of Columbia: The National Academies Press.

Bureau of Justice Statistics. 2014. http://www.bjs.gov/index.cfm?ty=ns#.

Bureau of Justice Statistics Recidivism. 2014. http://www.bjs.gov/index.cfm?ty=datool&surl=/recidivism/index.cfm.

"CASEL—Collaborative for Academic, Social, and Emotional Learning." 2018. *Theory of Action.* https://casel.org/in-the-schools.

Clandinin, D. J. and F. M. Connolly. 2001. *Narrative Inquiry: Experience and Story in Qualitative Research.* San Francisco: Jossey-Bass.

Coley, R., and P. Barton. 2006. *Locked Up and Lock Out: An Educational Perspective on the US Prison Population.* Policy information report to the policy information center ETS. Princeton, NJ. From Eric. ED496101.

"CommGap: Communication for Governance and Accountability Program." *Theories of Behavior Change.* http://documents.worldbank.org/curated/en/456261468164982535/Theories-of-behavior-change.

Cooper, A., M. Durose, and H. Snyder. 2014. "Recidivism of Prisoners Released in 30 States in 2005: Patterns from 2005 to 2010." Bureau of Justice Statistics. Washington, District of Columbia. http://www.bjs.gov/index.cfm?ty=pbdetail&iid=4986.

Creswell, J. W. 2012. *Educational Research: Planning, Conducting, and Evaluating Quantitative and Qualitative Research* (4th ed.). Upper Saddle River, NJ: Pearson Education.

Csikszentmihalyi, M. 1990. *Flow: The Psychology of Optimal Experience.* New York: Harper & Row. www.youtube.com/watch?v=fXIeFJCqsPs.

Davis, L. 2013. "Educational and Vocational Training in Prisons Reduces Recidivism, Improves Job Outlook." Rand Corporation press release. https://www.rand.org/news/press/2013/08/22.htm.

Davis, L., R. Bozick, J. Steele, J. Saunders, and J. Miles. 2013. "Evaluating the Effectiveness of Correctional Education: A Meta-Analysis of Programs That Provide Education to Incarcerated Adults." https://www.rand.org/pubs/research_reports/RR266.html.

Davis, L., J. Steele, R. Bozick, M. Williams, S. Turner, J. Miles, and P. Steinberg. 2014. "How Effective Is Correctional Education and Where Do We Go from Here?" Rand Corporation. https://www.rand.org/pubs/research_reports/RR564.html#download.

Desir, E., and C. L. Whitehead. 2010. "Motivational Strategies for Correctional Practitioners." In *Proceedings of the Ninth Annual College of Education and GSN Research Conference*, edited by M. S. Plakhotnik, S. M. Nielsen, and D. M. Pane, 12–17. Miami: Florida International University.

D'Andrea, C. 2010. "Tennessee's High School Dropouts: Examining the Fiscal Consequences." The Foundation for Educational Choice. http://files.eric.ed.gov/fulltext/ED517464.pdf.

DelliCarpini, M. 2010. "Building a Better Life: Implementing a Career and Technical Education Program for Incarcerated Youth." *The Journal of Correctional Education* 61, no. 4: 283–285. https://ceanational.org/journal.

DuFour, R., R. DuFour, and R. Eaker. 2008. *Revisiting Professional Learning Communities at Work*. Bloomington, IN: Solution Tree Press.

DuFour, R., R. DuFour, R. Eaker, and T. Many. 2010. *Learning by Doing: A Handbook for Professional Learning Communities at Work*, 2nd ed. Bloomington, IN: Solution Tree Press.

Dweck, C. 2006. *Mindset: The New Psychology of Success*. New York: Ballantine Books.

Esperian, J. H. 2010. "The Effect of Prison Education Programs on Recidivism." *Journal of Correctional Education* 61, no. 4: 316. https://ceanational.org/journal.

Fiester, L. 2010. *Early Warning! Why Reading by the End of Third Grade Matters?* Baltimore, MD: The Annie E. Casey Foundation. https://eric.ed.gov/?id=ED509795.

Florida Department of Correction Annual Report on Grade Level Equivalency. 2011. https://floridaliteracy.org/refguide/LITERACY%20AND%20CORRECTIONS%202011 %20-%20final.pdf.

Glaze, L. E., and L. M. Maruschak. 2008. "Parents in Prison and Their Minor Children." Bureau of Justice Statistics Special Report. Washington, DC: U.S. Department of Justice. http://www.bjs.gov/content/pub/pdf/pptmc.pdf.

Goss, R. 2011. "Getting the Message Across." *Adults Learning* 23, no. 2: 42–43.

Hall, R., and J. Killacky. 2008. "Correctional Education from the Perspective of the Prisoner Student." *The Journal of Correctional Education* 59, no. 4: 301–320. https://ceanational.org/journal.

Hairston, C. F. 2007. *Focus on Children with Incarcerated Parents*. Baltimore, MD: The Annie E. Casey Foundation, 14–25. http://www.f2f.ca.gov/res/pdf/FocusOnChildrenWith.pdf.

Harlow, C. W. 2003. "Education and Correctional Populations: Special Report" (NCJ 195670). Washington, DC. US Department of Justice, Office of Justice Programs. http://www.ojp.usdoj.gov/bjs.

Hattie, J. 2012. *Visible Learning for Teachers*. New York: Routledge.

Hattie, J., &and G. Yates. 2014. *Visible Learning and the Science of How We Learn*. New York: Routledge.

Henrichson, C., and R. Delaney. 2012. *The Price of Prisons: What Incarceration Costs Taxpayers*. New York: Vera Institute of Justice.

Hernandez, D. 2011. *Double Jeopardy: How Third-Grade Reading Skills and Poverty Influence High School Graduation*. Baltimore, MD: The Annie E. Casey Foundation. https://eric.ed.gov/?id=ED518818.

Huitt, W., and C. Dawson. 2011. "Social Development: Why It Is Important and How to Impact It." *Educational Psychology Interactive*. Valdosta, GA: Valdosta State University. http://www.edpsycinteractive.org/papers/socdev.pdf.

Kensit, D. A. 2010. "Rogerian Theory: A Critique of the Effectiveness of Pure Client-Centred Therapy." *Counselling Psychology Quarterly* 13, no. 4: 345–351. doi:10.1080/713658499.

Kotter, J. P. 2012. *Leading Change*. Boston, MA: Harvard Business Review.

Krueger, R. A. 2010. "Using Stories in Evaluation." In *Handbook of Practical Program Evaluation*, 3rd edition, edited by J. Wholey, H. Hatry, and K. Newcomer, 404–423. San Francisco, CA: Jossey-Bass.

Lincoln, Y. S., and E. G. Guba. 1985. *Naturalistic Inquiry*. Newbury Park, CA: Sage.

Lochner, L., and E. Moretti. 2001. "The Effect of Education on Crime: Evidence from Prison Inmates, Arrests, and Self-Reports." https://files.eric.ed.gov/fulltext/ED463346.pdf.

Martin, D., and K. Joomis. 2007. *Building Teachers: A Constructivist Approach to Introducing Education*. Belmont, CA: Wadsworth.

Maslow, A. 1943. "A Theory of Human Motivation." *Psychological Review* 50: 370–396. http://psychclassics.yorku.ca/Maslow/motivation.htm.

Maxwell, J. 2005. *Qualitative Research Design: An Interactive Approach*, 2nd edition. Thousand Oaks, CA: Sage.

McCornack, S. 2016. *Reflect & Relate*. Boston, MA: Bedford/St. Martin's.

McIntosh, P. 1990. *White Privilege: Unpacking the Invisible Knapsack*. National SEED Project on Inclusive Curriculum. www.nationalseedproject.org/images/documents/Knapsack_plus_Notes-Peggy_McIntosh.pdf.

Merriam, S. B. 1998. *Qualitative Research and Case Study Applications in Education*. San Francisco, CA: Jossey-Bass.

———. 2009. *Qualitative Research: A Guide to Design and Implementation*. San Francisco, CA: Jossey-Bass.

Miner-Romanoff, K. 2014. "Student Perceptions of Juvenile Offender Accounts in Criminal Education." *The American Journal of Criminal Justice* 39, no. 3: 611–629.

Moeller, M., S. L. Day, and B. D. Rivera. 2004. "How Is Education Perceived on the Inside? A Preliminary Study of Adult Males in a Correctional Setting." *Journal of Correctional Education* 55, no. 1: 40–59. https://ceanational.org/journal.

Mosley, E. 2008. "Incarcerated—Children of Parents in Prison Impacted." Texas Department of Criminal Justice. https://www.tdcj.state.tx.us/gokids/gokids_articles_children_impacted.html.

Muhammad A. 2015. *Overcoming the Achievement Gap Trap*. Bloomington, IN: Solution Tree Press.

Nally, J. M., S. Lockwood, T. Ho, and K. Knutson. 2014. "Post-Release Recidivism and Employment Among Different Types of Released Offenders: A 5-Year Follow-Up Study in the United States." *International Journal of Criminal Justice Sciences* 9, no. 1, 16–34. http://www.sascv.org/ijcjs/.

Nelson, L., and D. Lind. 2015. "The School to Prison Pipeline, Explained." *Vox*. https://www.vox.com.

Pajares, F. 2002. "Gender and Perceived Self-Efficacy in Self-Regulated Learning." *Theory into Practice* 41: 116–125. http://dx.doi.org/10.1207/s15430421tip4102_8.

Patton, M. 2015. *Qualitative Research & Evaluation Methods*, (4th ed.). Thousand Oaks, CA: Sage.

Perry, C. L., T. Barnowski, and G. S. Parcel. 1990. *How Individuals, Environments, and Health Behavior Interact: Social Learning Theory*. San Francisco, CA: Jossey-Bass.

Peshawaria, R. 2011. *Too Many Bosses, Too Few Leaders: Three Essential Principles You Need to Become an Extraordinary Leader*. New York, NY: Free Press.

Pettit, M. 2012. "Exemplary educational programs in Norwegian prisons: A case study of Norwegian educators' attitudes and humanitarian practices." Doctoral dissertation. ProQuest Dissertations and Theses database (UMI No. 3529614).

Pettit, M., and M. Kroth. 2011. "Educational Services in Swedish Prisons: Successful Programs of Academic and Vocational Training." *Criminal Justice Studies* 24, no. 3: 215–225.

Pink, D. 2009. *Drive*. New York, NY: Riverhead Books.

Raskin, N. J., C. R. Rogers, and M. C. Witty. 2008. "Client-Centered Therapy." In *Current Psychotherapies* (eighth ed.), edited by R. J. Corsini, D. Wedding, and F. Dumont, 141–186. Belmont, CA: Thomson Brooks/Cole.

Reeves, D. 2016. *From Leading to Succeeding: The Seven Elements of Effective Leadership in Education*. Bloomington, IN: Solution Tree Press.

Riley, J. 2014. *Please Stop Helping Us: How Liberals Make It Harder for Blacks to Succeed*. New York, NY: Encounter Books.

Rogers, C. R. 1957. "The Necessary and Sufficient Conditions of Therapeutic Personality Change." *Journal of Consulting Psychology* 21: 95–103.

Rossiter, M. 2007. "Possible Selves: An Adult Education Perspective." *New Directions for Adult and Continuing Education* 114: 5–15.

Ruiz, D. M. 1997. *The Four Agreements*. San Rafael, CA: Amber-Allen.

Safir, S. 2016. "5 Keys to Challenging Implicit Bias." *Edutopia*. www.edutopia.org/blog/keys-to-challenging-implicit-bias-shane-safir.

Sagor, R. 2000. *Guiding School Improvement with Action Research*. Alexandria, VA: ASCD.

Schmid, M. 2002. "The Eye of God: Religious Beliefs and Punishment in Early Nineteenth Century Prison Reform." *Theology Today* 59, no. 4: 546–558.

Schunk, D. 2016. *Learning Theories: An Educational Perspective*, 7th ed. Upper Saddle River, NJ: Pearson.

Shippers, M., D. Houchins, S. Crites, N. Derzis, and D. Patterson. 2010. "An Examination of Reading Skills of Incarcerated Males." *American Association of Adult and Continuing Learning* 21, no. 3–4: 4–12.

Sinek, S. 2011. *Start with Why: How Great Leaders Inspire Everyone to Take Action*. New York, NY: Penguin.

Skrla, L., K. McKenzie, and J. Scheurich. 2009. *Using Equity Audits to Create Equitable and Excellent Schools*. Thousand Oaks, CA: Corwin.

Sowell, T. 2005. *Black Rednecks and White Liberals*. San Francisco, CA: Encounter Books.

Spradley, J. P. 1980. *Participant Observation*. Fort Worth, TX: Harcourt Brace Jovanovich College.

Steele, S. 2006. *White Guilt*. New York, NY: Harper Collins.

——. 1990. *The Content of Our Character*. New York, NY: Harper Perennial.

Strauss, A., and J. Corbin. 1990. *Basics of Qualitative Research: Grounded Theory Procedures and Techniques*. Newbury Park, CA: Sage.

Suttie, J. 2016. "Four Ways Teachers Can Reduce Implicit Bias." *Greater Good Magazine*. https://greatergood.berkeley.edu/article/item/four_ways_teachers_can_reduce_implicit_bias.

Vigne, N., E. Davis, and D. Brazzell. 2008. *Broken Bonds: Understanding and Addressing the Needs of Children with Incarcerated Parents*. Washington, DC: Urban Institute Justice Policy Center, 1–14.

https://www.urban.org/sites/default/files/publication/31486/411616-Broken-Bonds-Understanding-and-Addressing-the-Needs-of-Children-with-Incarcerated-Parents.PDF.

Wagner, T. 2008. *The Global Achievement Gap*. New York, NY: Basic Books.

Wigfield A., and J. Eccles. 2000. "Expectancy-Value Theory of Achievement Motivation." *Contemporary Educational Psychology* 25: 68–81. https://doi.org/10.1006/ceps.1999.1015.

Wilkinson, B. 2002. *The Prayer of Jabez*. Sisters, OR: Multnomah.

Willingham, D. 2009. *Why Don't Students Like School*. San Francisco, CA: Jossey-Bass.

APPENDIX A

Pilot Study: Questions for the Individuals at the DCSO Training Facility

1) What is creativity?
2) Are you born with creativity?
3) Can creativity be learned?
4) Can creativity be lost?
5) Did your public school education teach you creativity?
6) What were your experiences, good or bad, with your educational experience?
7) What was your experience with other students?
8) What was your experience with administrators?
9) If a problem did occur, how did the school handle the situation?
10) How did your parents get involved with the school?
11) How did they help you?
12) What were your initial expectations for attending school?
13) What are your expectations now?

APPENDIX B

Research Questionnaire

1) What were the criminal offenses that you were involved in school?
2) What criminal activities led to your incarceration?
3) We know what you did to get incarcerated and how you did it, but what is the reason? What do you think is the reason *why*?
4) What was the demographics of your community (family, income, community, church)?
5) What grade did you complete when you dropped out of school? What was the reason to drop out of school?
6) What were some of the positive experiences you had in the public school system?
7) What was your favorite subject and why?
8) What was your least-favorite subject in school and why?
9) What kind of problems or negative experiences did you encounter that you did not expect?
10) What were your perceptions of other students' initial reaction to you, and did that lead to your mindset of how you should react to school?
11) If an academic problem occurred, did the school support you both personally in school and outside of school? (Please circle)
Almost always   **Often**   **Sometimes**   **Seldom**   **Never**
Explain by describing the situation.
12) If a social problem occurred, did the school support you personally and as a student? (Please circle) **Almost always**   **Often**   **Sometimes**   **Seldom**   **Never**
Explain by describing the incidents.
13) What kind of positive collaboration or interaction did you have with other teachers or administrators? (Please circle)
Almost always   **Often**   **Sometimes**   **Seldom**   **Never**
Explain by describing the incidents.
14) What kind of negative collaboration or interaction did you have with teachers or administrators? (Please circle)
Almost always   **Often**   **Sometimes**   **Seldom**   **Never**
Explain by describing the incidents.
15) What were the positive interaction you had with other students? (Please circle)
Almost always   **Often**   **Sometimes**   **Seldom**   **Never**
Explain by describing the incidents.

16) What were the negative interactions you had with other students? (Please circle)
Almost always   **Often**   **Sometimes**   **Seldom**   **Never**
Explain by describing the incidents.
17) What extracurricular activities did you participate in during your school experience and why?
(Please circle) **Almost always**   **Often**   **Sometimes**   **Seldom**   **Never**
Explain by describing the incidents.

APPENDIX C

Research Questionnaire Responses

1) What were the criminal offenses that you were involved in school?

    a) Theft
    b) Drugs, smoking pot, alcohol
    c) Drug distribution
    d) Prostitution and pole dancing at the age of fourteen in adult clubs
    e) Curfew violation
    f) Trespassing
    g) Fighting
    h) Skipping school

2) What criminal activities led to your incarceration?

    a) Prostitution
    b) Selling drugs
    c) Burglary, theft, of merchandise
    d) DWI
    e) Possession and using drugs (cocaine and meth)
    f) Assault with deadly weapon
    g) The rush of stealing
    h) Driving with no license, parole violation, and evading arrest
    i) Violation of probation by using drugs

3) We know what you did to get incarcerated and how you did it, but what is the reason? What do you think is the reason?

    a) "I did not know that I could take my child to the hospital without insurance or money. I had to do something and that was stealing."
    b) "My addiction."
    c) "Drug use…addiction and knowing only one way to live."
    d) "I was trying to return the items for a girlfriend and got caught."
    e) "Bad lifestyle—influence from my friends."
    f) "Because of the rush I got from stealing."

g) "Because I had a drug problem, and when I take certain drugs, it makes do things I shouldn't."

h) "Because I had been up for many days and could not think straight."

i) "I wanted to have a family and did not want to be alone."

j) "I was drunk and using drugs."

k) "I think the reason why I was getting high was to feel more accepted within my own skin. Also I like to party, and the feeling of drugs gave me and made me feel really excited hyped up and fun."

l) "Because I am an addict and was trying to self-medicate in order to numb my feelings to hide the pain I was dealing with."

4) What was the demographics of your community (family, income, community, church)?

a) "My father passed away when I was seven years old. Before, he wrote songs and plays. He composed music. He also played the saxophone and the piano. My mother was a jazz singer, and I grew up going with her to singing jobs. She taught me to carry myself as a lady and that the show must always go on and never let anyone see you sweat. We moved around a lot and didn't go to church, although my mother taught us about the Lord and pretty much instilled Jesus into us. We traveled around, and I was one of four black students in the rural area of Michigan."

b) "Inner City Nashville—bad area. My mother and grandmother got locked up, so I had to take care of my little sister and brother. I dropped out of school and started selling drugs to support my sister and brother."

c) "Family of fourteen, low income, and very poor community, but we attended church."

d) "My family is a close family with a decent income. We lived in a drug zone, but there were churches there.'"

e) "I am trying to rebuild my relationship with my mother, my sister, and my kids. The area is low income with a lot of drugs being sold in the open.

f) "A nine-people household, low-income area, but we were getting by. My family were members of the Jehovah Witness Church."

g) "My mom worked in a bank, and my father was a preacher. We lived in Bexar County, Texas, in San Antonio."

h) "I went to church with my grandmother. My mother was an alcoholic. My father was a workaholic and was murdered when I was murdered when I was in the ninth grade."

i) "My mother and sisters, no one else. Poor neighborhood and infested with gangs."

j) "Lower middle-class homes, big church within a mile of my home."

5) What grade did you complete when you dropped out of school? What was the reason to drop out of school?

a) "Second semester of my senior year. I had to move out of the house and could not stay in school because I had to work to pay for my rent of my own place. I was an honor student and took AP classes, but was overwhelmed when I left home."

b) "Eleventh grade because of drugs."

c) "Tenth grade. I had no incentive to stay. My boyfriend already graduated."

d) "Eleventh grade. I got married."
e) "Fourth grade, running the streets and had to find different ways to make money."
f) "Ninth grade. My father was murdered and no mother."
g) "Tenth grade due to drugs."
h) "Eleventh grade because I had a baby."
i) "Eighth grade, dropped out 'cause of drugs."
j) "Ninth. Bored."
k) "Got credit for ninth grade, but I went to the twelfth grade."
l) "I completed ninth grade but dropped out because of too much pressure from the school."
m) "Ninth grade, and I got pregnant."
n) "I was in the beginning of the tenth grade when I stopped going to school. I ran away from where I was living. I moved to Nashville, and I tried to enroll into Maplewood HS but fail in the attempts when I kept getting the run around about getting my transcripts from out of state."
o) "Beginning of the ninth grade. Got bored."

6) What were some of the positive experiences you had in the public-school system?

a) "None."
b) "I very much enjoyed being in the play *Grease*. I played Sandy. I was really excited about that. That is something that sticks out a lot to me. I also enjoyed being a cheerleader, and I loved running track as well."
c) "Some of the teachers."
d) "Trying to make friends."
e) "Diverse community and different cultures."
f) "Never went to school."
g) "Good parents, cheerleading, and good grades."
h) "I am not sure. I skipped a lot."
i) "First through seventh. I really liked and loved to learn. After that, drugs took over, and I hated it and dropped out."
j) "Challenging class and plenty of after school programs."

7) What was your favorite subject and why?

a) "I had two favorite classes. I enjoyed most sciences; my favorite was Biology II. It was an honors class, so it kept me interested and was more challenging. I also liked Latin II. Although it is considered to be a dead language, I have read that it is still used, especially in the medical field."
b) "Math and English—made good grades."
c) "Reading, I did well in it."
d) "English—It came natural."
e) "Did not have one."
f) "Reading, I loved to read."
g) "Math, because I loved numbers."
h) "English, it was easy for me."

    i)   "Social Studies. It tells you real stuff."

    j)   "None"

    k)   "Math 'cause I loved to count money."

    l)   "Math. It is universal."

    m)   "English, I loved to write."

    n)   "Reading and writing. They were my favorite because I always enjoyed putting words together and reading."

8) What was your least favorite subject in school and why?

    a)   "Math could never understand it."

    b)   "Reading, because I don't like to do a lot of reading."

    c)   "My least favorite class was math. This is because I had trouble solving problems and remembering the formulas."

    d)   "Math. Can't really get it. It's hard for me to understand sometimes."

    e)   "Math. It is difficult for me."

    f)   "Writing/language arts and reading. English is a difficult language."

    g)   "Math. I can't understand it."

    h)   "Social studies. It was hard to understand."

    i)   "Social studies because it was boring and made no sense."

    j)   "Math. I was slower at learning than other students, and the teacher did not help me."

    k)   "Science. Confusing."

    l)   "My least favorite class was chemistry. I had a teacher that was not interested in teaching. She repeatedly told us that she would not answer any questions and not to bother her because she was pregnant and didn't feel good."

9) What kind of problems or negative experiences did you encounter that you did not expect?

    a)   "My Spanish, geometry, Latin II, and chemistry teachers all let their personal lives disrupt their ability to teach, and we were not held accountable, at least as far as I could tell. It made learning hard for me as I had to teach myself. That is okay in college, but not in high school."

    b)   "Bad influences and bullies."

    c)   "Man getting shot."

    d)   "My parents getting divorced and me having a baby at a young age."

    e)   "Love and a baby."

    f)   "I moved around a lot, so I went to many different schools, and it was hard to have any structure or stability."

    g)   "One big problem that I would encounter in school a lot was being picked on a lot. Also, I didn't ask for help when I needed it. The teachers did offer either. I would smoke weed a lot before school, during and after school, so that would prevent me from able to focus in class."

    h)   "Negative attitudes from other students."

10) What were your perceptions of other students' initial reaction to you, and did that lead to your mindset of how you should react to school?

   a) "I was usually talked about because of my clothes."
   b) "I stayed to myself and ignored anything that came my way, and I kept my head high."
   c) "I always felt as if people didn't like me, so this made me feel scared a lot and drawn to myself."
   d) "Tried to keep up with the crowd."
   e) "I should have acted better."
   f) "They liked me, so it was okay."
   g) "I didn't talk to a lot of other students. I felt way ahead of them and didn't fit in. I hung out with older students."
   h) "Because of them, I did not want to attend school at all."
   i) "Didn't get along with many students."
   j) "I was never very social. They thought that I was 'stuck up' because of that. I had less than five friends, and they were really only acquaintances. My mindset was affected by that. I threw myself into schoolwork and an after-school job. I did not enjoy school."

11) If an academic problem occurred, did the school support you both personally in school and outside of school? (Please circle)

Almost always	Often	Sometimes	Seldom	Never.
3		5	2	7

Explain by describing the situation:

   a) "I never had a social problem that would have required their involvement."
   b) "Only when they made time."
   c) "I didn't get involved with school."
   d) "I dropped out in the ninth grade. No motivation to stay."
   e) "My teachers always wanted me to stay after school and do extra work."
   f) "My mother would try to help me."
   g) "They were not involved."
   h) "I hardly went to school."
   i) "Bullying was a big problem, but the school did not believe it was happening."
   j) "Never."
   k) "I would not express to the teachers that I had a problem."
   l) "I got pregnant in the eighth grade, and no one supported me."

12) If a social problem occurred, did the school support you personally and as a student? (Please circle)

Almost always	Often	Sometimes	Seldom	Never
1		6	4	6

Explain by describing the incidents.

   a) "I received no help."
   b) "I get along with everyone, and if there was a problem, we would talk it over with one another."

c) "I got into some trouble outside of school and got kicked off of the cheerleading team."
d) "Never."
e) "One teacher was really concerned about the abuse with a man who raised me but could not help me or guide me to the people who could. I guess he just didn't want to get involved."
f) "I stopped going to school for depression. They wanted to only know why I was depressed but offered no help."
g) "My principal didn't like me."
h) "Only if we got caught."
i) "If I made it a serious problem."

13) What kind of positive collaboration or interaction did you have with other teachers or administrators? (Please circle)

Almost always	Often	Sometimes	Seldom	Never
1	1	6	5	4

Explain by describing the incidents.

a) "I did see some teachers doing special projects with students. I wasn't one of them, mostly by my choice."
b) "I needed special help but seldom got it."
c) "One teacher knew I had problems at home."
d) "My fourth grade teacher was my piano teacher. I was almost always liked by my teachers."
e) "Sometimes we would we had a voluntary class for helping the homeless. It made me look at life differently."
f) "Never."
g) "I usually stayed to myself and didn't really talk to my teachers or anyone."
h) "Usually negative experiences."

14) What kind of negative collaboration or interaction did you have with teachers or administrators? (Please circle)

Almost always	Often	Sometimes	Seldom	Never
	5	5	3	4

Explain by describing the incidents.

a) "Sometimes. Usually negative."
b) "Sometimes, because they knew I was a terrible mother outside of school."
c) "In middle school, my gym teacher called me an alien, as in someone from another country."
d) "Often, because I would fight a lot."
e) "I had a teacher that was very mean to me because he was a racist. I am not just being funny about it."
f) "Often. In tenth grade, I had problems."
g) "My Spanish, geometry, Latin II, and chemistry teachers all let their personal lives disrupt their ability to teach, and we were not held accountable, at least as far as I could tell. It made learning hard for me as I had to teach myself. That is okay in college, but not in high school."

15) What were the positive interactions you had with other students? (Please circle)

Almost always	Often	Sometimes	Seldom	Never
2	3	5	5	2

Explain by describing the incidents.

a) "Often. We were encouraged to work together in groups per projects or in art class. Sometimes we would pick our own groups, sometimes we didn't. My groups met up at each other's house, church, or a park to do our work depending on the project."
b) "Never."
c) "Extracurricular activities. School football games."
d) "I wasn't very positive. I was into drugs and boys at a young age."
e) "I loved gymnastics and cheerleading. Hung out with pretty good people."
f) "My middle school teacher helped me out with my English and other students, and then we would help each other."
g) "I had few friends in school, but the ones I had we got along very well."

16) What were the negative interactions you had with other students? (Please circle)

Almost always	Often	Sometimes	Seldom	Never
2	5	7		3

Explain by describing the incidents.

a) "Never accepted, except by the gangs."
b) "I was picked on and bullied a lot."
c) "Almost always. We always do stuff we were not supposed to do, and keeping up with the crowd got me into trouble."
d) "People are mean—plain and simple."
e) "I stayed in trouble."
f) "Fighting, arguing, gangs, and drugs."
g) "I had an older boyfriend, and his older friends got me into drugs and doing things that I shouldn't do."
h) "Kids are kids. They always make fun of people because something they said or did, etc."

17) What extracurricular activities did you participate in during your school experience and why? (Please circle)

Almost always	Often	Sometimes	Seldom	Never
	1	4	2	10

Explain by describing the incidents:

a) "I played basketball fifth to tenth grade, soccer eleventh grade, and third grade I played baseball. Girl Scouts first to the fourth grades. Latin Club in the tenth grade. I always enjoyed sports. My mother really pushed me to be active after school, so I had to be involved in something. I also went to church at least twice a week. Those activities kept me out of trouble and forced me to be more organized."
b) "Never."
c) "Football games, basketball tryouts."

d) "I did not want to. My extra activities were drugs and being in a gang."

e) "PE softball."

f) "Never had support from my foster parents."

g) "I loved doing extracurricular activities when I attended school. I played basketball, I ran track, and I was a cheerleader."

h) "Cosmetology, because I love to do hair."

Follow-up comments by students:

a) "My whole life was a mess, starting as a kid, as early as six years old. I moved around a lot due to my mother's drug addiction. Missed a lot of schooling, but somewhere I learned to read, and I thank God for that."

b) "The ladies in the office always called the man who raised me when I went to them about the abuse at home, which always caused more abuse once I got home from school."

c) "I need my GED. I am trying really hard, 'cause back then I didn't even try. No one told me why I needed an education, and the school just passed me on."

d) "Ultimately, I left school in my senior year. I dropped out because I was overworked. I felt that I never had time to be a kid, develop who I was, find hobbies, etc. I was always in the most advanced classes my school offered, in after-school programs, church, or work. There was no time for me. My grandmother tried to be my mother. My mother was more focused on her career and personal goals. There was always a lot of tension in the house, and I felt I didn't have any support. Like I said, my grandmother tried, but she wasn't my mother. My grandmother was born in 1920 and just could not relate to me and what I was going through. My school never realized what I was also going through either."

e) "I hated school, but I really wanted to like it. I was like the picture of the shark fin and goldfish you showed in class. I was bold on the top like the shark fin but a scared goldfish on the bottom. I couldn't show anyone how much I needed help. If I did, I would have shown signs of weakness. I wish someone would have been there to help me overcome my feelings of insecurity. I wish someone would have told me about the importance of education and how it could get me out of the mess that I am in. I wish I had someone whom I could talk to and not make me feel like a criminal. I wish I had someone who would just listen to me and not judge me." *Note: This student came up to me after the focus-group session and asked to have her questionnaire back so she could add a final comment.*

APPENDIX D

Methodology of Research Questionnaire:
Codes, Categories, Themes, Theory

Code

1) In vivo: actual language of the participants
2) Process coding: action coding
3) Initial coding: breaking down data into discrete units
4) Emotion coding: recalling the experiences
5) Values coding: reflecting on attitudes, values, and beliefs
6) Versus coding: us versus them

Categories

1) Educational experience
2. Teachers and administration
3) Individual
4) Attitudes
5) Acceptance
6) Interaction with education both negative and positive
7) Resources
8) Expectations
9) Perceptions
10) Parental relation
11) Ethnicity
12) Demographics

Themes

1) Hard work pays off.
2) People want to be needed.
3) Good teachers make a difference.
4) Bad teachers make a difference.
5) Purpose makes a difference.

6) Drugs destroy.
7) Parental impact makes a difference.
8) Diversity has an impact.
9) Not playing the victim card.
10) Individual responsibility.

Theory

Education experiences do influence the criminality of an individual, but the main factor is the lack of or proper parental, community, and individual involvement

APPENDIX E

Adapted for this research study:
The Life Skills Development Program for the High School Equivalency Diploma

The Davidson County Sheriff's Office
Purpose, Value, and Parenting

Handbook

By Tom Hallquist
June 1, 2016

I want to give recognition and a special thank-you to Paul J. Mulloy, Director of Programs, for the DCSO, W.S. Jamieson (Chaplain Scott), Mario Allen of the Fatherhood Development Training Program, Awana Lifeline—*Inmate Challenge*, Rajeev Peshawaria, author of *Too Many Bosses and Too Few Leaders*.

The Purpose and Value Development Program

The purpose and value development program is a new class offered at the DCSO Harding Place facility. The class is a six-week life-skill course designed to help inmates deepen their relationships with their children by understanding their own purpose and values. Whether the inmates have no current contact with their children or frequent contact, this program is intended to guide oneself to examine the underlying beliefs about what it means to be a positive member of society and how to navigate to a more meaningful role with their family and support group. By helping understand one's strengths, overcome the lack of effective role models, and develop the necessary skills to be an increasingly effective member of society, the program will offer support, encouragement, and resources to achieve this objective. The main goals of this program are the following:

1. Strengthen and support good parenting by
    - recognizing strengths and potential by developing a sense of purpose,
    - establishing values that will guide one's purpose,
    - overcoming a sense of guilt by using your experiences as a positive learning tool,
    - increasing knowledge and skills,

- providing information about resources,
- using opportunities for positive interaction with one's support group.

2. Improve the parent-child relationship by
   - using time-positive activities to interact with family,
   - helping parents to communicate better with their children.

3. Reduce the cycle of incarceration.

4. Become a positive role model by developing a positive purpose in life and values to guide that purpose.

Prayer of Jabez

Jabez cried out to the Lord of Israel, Oh that You would bless me and enlarge my territory! Let your hand be with me and keep me from evil so that I will not cause pain. And God granted his request. (1 Chronicles 4:10)

Introduction

In the past twenty years, there has been an unprecedented growth of incarceration in the United States. Currently, there are more than two million adults in prison. What is often overlooked by the criminal justice system in the United States is the relationship between inmates and their families. According to Barbara Bosley, Christie Donner, Caroline McLean, and Ellen Toomey-Hale in their book *Parenting from Prison*, "The majority of women and men in prison are parents of children under the age of 18." There can be many emotional, financial, and legal issues that arise when a parent is incarcerated. Understanding how children are impacted is very important for the parent and extended families. It is often stated that when a parent is incarcerated, the children also "do the time." Although many children who have a parent in prison adjust and go on to live very successful lives, it has to be noted that children who have parents in prison are more likely to have difficulty in school, both academically and socially. Children who have a parent in prison are more likely to engage in substance abuse, delinquency, and gang-related activities. Children who have a parent in prison are often traumatized from separation. This course is designed to assist the inmate to further enhance parenting skills and to develop positive interactions. Being incarcerated does not mean one has to give up their rights to be a parent or that the relationship with their children becomes less important. It does allow one the opportunity to become a positive mentor and role model for their children.

Schedule

Week 1

Lesson 1: Getting Acquainted and Setting Norms and Goals
Lesson 1.1: Understanding Purpose and Values
Lesson 1.2: Overcoming Guilt and Shame

Week 2

Lesson 2: "You are the Message"—Building Bridges, Not Walls
Lesson 2.1: How to Develop and Sustain Relationship with Your Support Group
Lesson 2.2: What Is Parenthood?

Week 3

Lesson 3: Communication Understanding Your Needs and the Needs of Your Children
Lesson 3.1: Problem Solving—Dealing with Behavioral Challenges

Week 4

Lesson 4: Age-Related Parenting Challenges
Lesson 4.1: Activities to Engage Children and Build Your Child's Self-Esteem
Lesson 4.2: Parents' Influence on Children

Week 5

Lesson 5: Relationships; Getting Help from Your Support Network
Lesson 5.1: Video Parenting from Prison
Lesson 5.1: Male/Female Relationships Discussion

Week 6

Lesson 6: Building a Legacy
Lesson 6.1: Review

Week 7

Lesson 7: Graduation

Session 1: Purpose and Values

Part 1: Self-Assessment—The Nine Questions You Might Want to Ask Yourself

The questions will help you define *purpose* and *values.*

1. What few things are most important to me?
2. Purpose—do I want to?
3. What results do I want to bring about or create?
4. How do I want people to experience me?
5. What values will *guide* my behavior?
6. What situations cause me to feel strong *emotions* or give me *energy*?
7. What are my strengths, weaknesses, opportunities, and threats (SWOT)?

8. How can I apply my strengths, weaknesses, opportunities, and threats to become a better parent?
9. How will I handle threats?

Session 2: Meaning of Parenthood

1. Define what the word *parent* means to you.
2. What is my cultures image of a parent?
3. Describe the characteristics of a good parent.
4. Describe what kind of parent you are now.
5. What kind of parent would you like to become?
6. Do you believe you can be a parent from jail/prison?

Session 3: Parent as a Provider

1. Were your parents' good providers?
2. What are some things that every parent should provide for their family?
3. What were some of the things in which you provided for your family?
4. What were some of the things in which you desired to give your family but were not able?
5. Do you believe you can provide for your family from jail/prison? Explain your answer.
6. Why do you believe a lot of people in prison stop providing for their families once they are incarcerated?

Session 3: Responsibilities

1. What is your definition of a soldier?
2. What are some sacrifices in which you have made for your family?
3. What are some sacrifices you knew you needed to make in the past but failed to do so?
4. Has anyone ever made sacrifices for you? If someone has, write their name(s). What type of sacrifices?
5. Why do you believe a person makes sacrificed for others?
6. What are some sacrifices in which you can make right now in your life for your family?

Session 4: Parenting Habits

1. What is your definition of a habit?
2. What are some habits in which you believe every father and mother should have?
3. What are some good habits you believe you possess as a father or mother?
4. How did you learn these good habits?
5. What are some bad habits you possess as a parent?
6. How did you learn these bad habits?

Session 5: Relationship

1. What were some good memories you had from your family?
2. How do you believe your incarceration has impacted your family?
3. What are some of the things you did to help your family?
4. What are some things you can do today to assist your extended family here in prison?
5. Explain how you can be a better person.
6. Explain how you can be a better person to your parents.
7. Explain how you will be an asset to your family.
8. Now what is your purpose?

APPENDIX F

Equity Audit Process

The purpose of the equity audits was to develop an understanding of the demographics of the community and academic achievement of the inmates. The equity audits were conducted to establish a foundation for the reasons for their behavior and if the educational experience influenced that behavior or mindset. Statistics were gathered to develop a picture of the demographics and to determine if any factor contributed to the educational competency that could have an impact on the problems in the community that relate to the students' academic achievement. The process began with community demographic studies to determine the ethnic and economic areas of criminal activity and academic ratings of the various school districts. The research material was obtained from public records and databases developed by the DCSO (see DCSO, Davidson County, and TN Gov sources).

Sources

- www.city-data.com/county/Davidson_County-TN.html
- https://www.nashville.gov/Police-Department/News-and-Reports/Crime-Statistics/Nashville-Crime-Statistics.aspx
- https://sci.ccc.nashville.gov/CrimeMap/Index
- https://www.tn.gov/education/data/data-downloads.html
- https://www.tn.gov/education/data/tcap-results-at-a-glance.html
- https://www.tn.gov/content/tn/education/data/department-reports/2017-annual-statistical-report.html

Davidson County, TN, Demographics

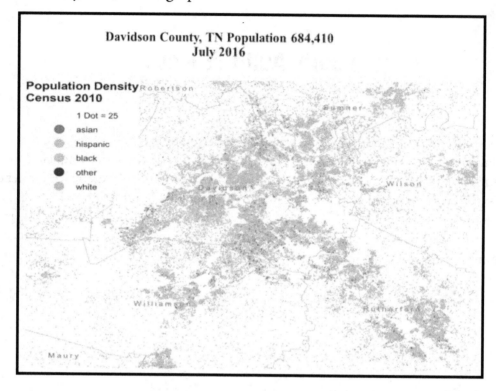

Davidson County Demographics July 2016

Population: 684,410
Median Age: 33.0
Males: 323,721 (48.4%)
Female: 344.626 (51.6%)
Median Income $51,000
17.6% Adult workforce earns less than $26,000/year
White Non-Hispanic 57.4%
Black Non-Hispanic 27.5%
Hispanic or Latino 9.8%
Asian 3.0%
Two or more races 1.9%

www.city-data.com/county/Davidson_County-TN.html

Metropolitan Nashville Police Department Eight Precinct Map and Crime Rate Areas

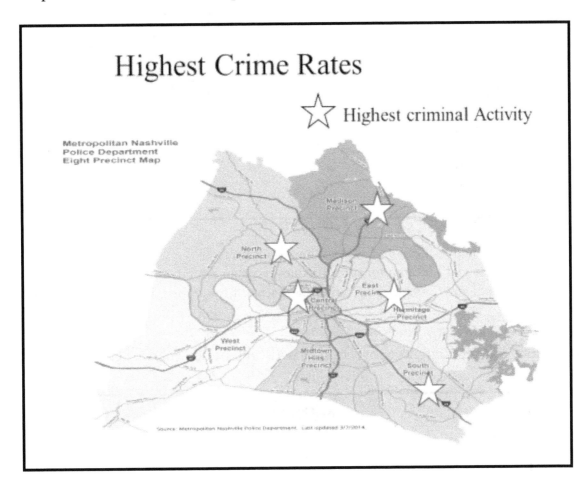

www.city-data.com/county/Davidson_County-TN.html

https://www.nashville.gov/Police-Department/News-and-Reports/Crime-Statistics/Nashville-Crime-Statistics.aspx

https://sci.ccc.nashville.gov/CrimeMap/Index

Davidson County, TN, School District Reports 2017

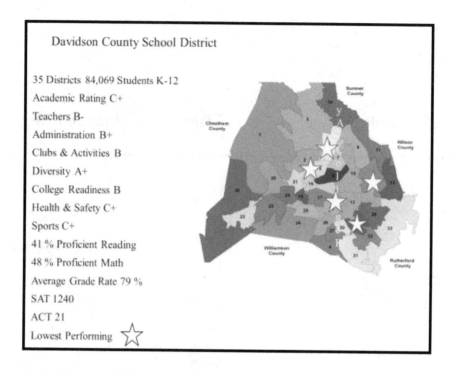

https://www.tn.gov/education/data/data-downloads.html
https://www.tn.gov/education/data/tcap-results-at-a-glance.html
https://www.tn.gov/content/tn/education/data/department-reports/2017-annual-statistical-report.html

Grade Level by Age Range Report from Davidson County Sheriff's Office Database

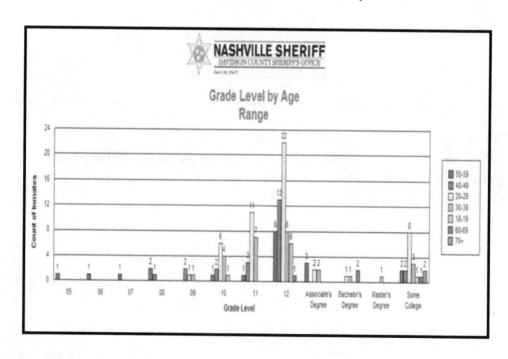

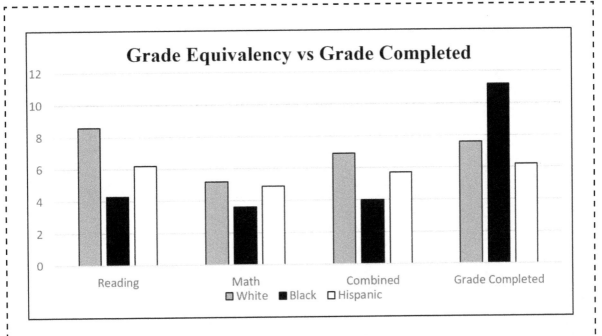

Grade Equivalency vs Grade Completed

Twenty-two females tested in March and April 2017 at the DCSO Training Facility and the DCSO Jail consisting of seven Caucasians, nine African Americans, and six Hispanics. The tests were conducted at the beginning of the sessions prior to classroom instruction. The scores are included in the risk ratio table.

Risk Ratio (.25 Difference is an area of concern)				
Reading	White / Black	(1.65)		
	White / Hispanic	(1.38)		
Math	White / Black	(1.19)		
	White / Hispanic	(0.89)		
Combined	White / Black	(1.72)		
	White / Hispanic	(1.21)		
Scores				
White	Reading	8.6	Math	5.2
Black	Reading	4.3	Math	3.6
Hispanic	Reading	6.2	Math	4.9

The equity audits became a leading agent of initiating change in the system by making individuals aware of the situation. The *Equity-Oriented Change Agent* (EOCA) became a guiding attribute to initiate a process of conversations and a course of action to develop a cooperative approach to the understanding of the problems and to develop positive outcomes for the incarcerated individual and the educational system (Skrla, 70–79).

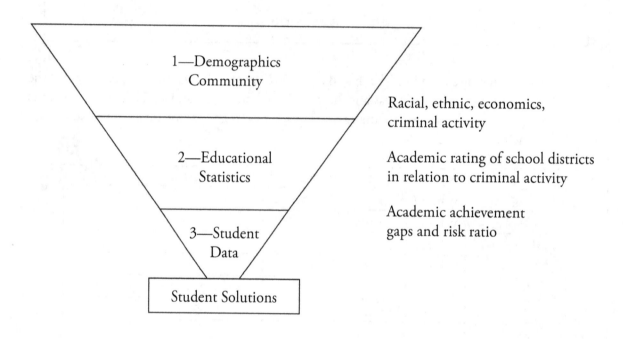

1—Demographics
Community

Racial, ethnic, economics,
criminal activity

2—Educational
Statistics

Academic rating of school districts
in relation to criminal activity

3—Student
Data

Academic achievement
gaps and risk ratio

Student Solutions

APPENDIX G

Permission to Adapt Basic Principle to Meet the Needs of This Research

Written Permission from John P. Kotter to adapt his eight stages in leadership from his book *Leading Change*.

From: John Kotter [john@kotterinc.com]
Sent: Friday, November 16, 2018 12:34 PM
To: Hallquist, Tom
Subject: Re: Leading Change

Tom,

This is marvelous work that you're doing. Good for you.

Thanks for asking for permission. Many people do not. You should go ahead and do whatever is helpful for your project and for the people who can benefit from it. All you need to do is just be truthful in your writing about where the model that you adapted came from and who developed it, with appropriate references.

We already have examples of people using the model not just for organizational change but for changing in small groups, even family. Someone taught a course in New York City and assigned "our iceberg is melting" as a reading. The instructor asked the students to write a paper based on the parable. One Korean American student wrote about how he thought the parable was silly when he read it until he actually applied it when they had a crisis in his family: his brother was threatening to drop out of high school. They followed the eight steps and, a good ending, his brother stayed in high school and went on to college. Years ago I was encouraged by someone who wanted me to turn this into a new kind of diet book which emphasizes not just food and nutrition (there are many possibilities here that will work just fine) but the real problem which is changing personal habits and sometimes even lifestyles and sustaining those changes. I didn't do it but I think it would make a great "diet" book. So the point is, you are onto something. Run with it.

JPK

Douglas Reeves, phone conversation on November 16, 2018. Oral permission granted to adapt his *From Leading to Succeeding: The Seven Elements of Effective Leadership in Education* to meet the needs of this research.

ABOUT THE AUTHOR

Dr. Tom Hallquist, is an associate professor of communication studies at Columbia State Community College, Columbia, Tennessee, and an adjunct professor at Belmont University, Nashville, Tennessee. Dr. Hallquist also is an instructor at the Davidson County Jails in Nashville and has also taught classes for the Tennessee Department of Corrections. Prison courses range from *Parenting from Prison*, *anger management*, *entrepreneurship*, *organization leadership*, and *GED* for the Davidson County Sheriff's Office. All of his classes, whether in prison or on the college campus, focus on practical, purposeful, and value-driven education. Dr. Hallquist is a motivational speaker and advisor for prison reform.

CPSIA information can be obtained
at www.ICGtesting.com
Printed in the USA
LVHW060304150321
681547LV00015B/75